HOW TO USE THE
TWELVE TISSUE SALTS

A Guide to the Biochemic Treatment

HOW TO USE THE
TWELVE TISSUE SALTS

A Guide to the Biochemic Treatment

With chapters on Balanced Diet,
Body's Need of Minerals and Vitamins

by
Editors of B. Jain

B. Jain Publishers (P) Ltd.
USA – EUROPE – INDIA

HOW TO USE THE TWELVE TISSUE SALTS

First Edition: 2009
3rd Impression: 2019

Published by Kuldeep Jain for
B. JAIN PUBLISHERS (P) LTD.
B. Jain House, D-157, Sector-63,
NOIDA-201307, U.P. (INDIA)
Tel.: +91-120-4933333 • *Email:* info@bjain.com
Website: **www.bjain.com**

Printed in India by
J.J. Offset Printers

ISBN: 978-81-319-0738-2

Publisher's Note

Today in the time of stress and busy lifestyle, every day we hear of a new disease being discovered. The more we move towards advancement, the more our sufferings are increasing. People are also trying to be more close to nature as they can be. All the alternative therapies are getting more recognization in the eyes of general public than ever. Biochemic system is also one of the healing system which is becoming one sought after system of medicine.

There was a need for a simple book on Biochemic for general public since long which they could use for the day-to-day illness. Our editorial team researched on all the literature available on Biochemic and have compiled this information for readers. We hope that the readers find this information useful for themselves and their family.

Kuldeep Jain
C.E.O., B. Jain Publishers

Introduction

The food we eat, produced by vegetable and animal life, consists of minerals which get absorbed into their fibres from simpler forms of chemical life. The plant takes up the minerals from the soil and the carbon from the atmosphere from which it embodies its own substance and the animals and fish eat plant and other forms of living organisms for their structural maintenance.

Human beings use this organic food in combination with the air they breathe and the water they drink for the various purposes needed for their physical tissues. The process of digestion and the correct assimilation of that food comprises of breaking down of organized material into its simpler constituents, amino-acids, sugar, mineral elements, carbon, hydrogen, and their absorption by the body tissues. When this operation proceeds normally throughout all its tissues, the body is in health. The ceaseless activity of this complicated process constitutes the body's metabolism.

Various diseases and injuries can disrupt, increase or lower a person's metabolism.

The cells of the human body are composed of inorganic and organic material. The intake of air, food and drink provides with these constituents.

The health of the physical tissue is also affected by the person's individuality, by the hopes, despairs, faiths or fears which dominate the mentality. In physical terms it is not possible to say of what hope and faith consist, but it is seen that these qualities inspire human beings and their effects on the physical plane cannot to be denied. The eye becomes brighter, the cheeks improve in color and vigor in some degree is increased, obviously a chemical change has affected the blood for a good purpose and in all healing this is a salient factor of great value.

Contents

CHAPTER 1

The Biochemic Nutrient Remedies

The biochemic nutrient remedies, which embrace also the Schüssler tissue salts, are inorganic mineral substance, the very same of which our earth and its soils are composed. When they are suitably selected and prepared and taken as remedies for various diseases or physical disturbances, a required food substance is being taken in a simpler form than the meals normally contain, thus requiring no breakdown of a complicated substance. This is a great advantage where the various links of the digestive process are weak or functionless. Disease invariably brings a disturbance in metabolism. Shrunken, thickened or weak conditions of cell life with disrupted functions or metabolism may be heightened and displaced as in fevers, injuries and inflammations.

Biochemic tissue remedies provide an immediate answer for both serious and slight disturbances, which when correctly diagnosed and treated should only require one other factor for success, the life-energy of the person taking this treatment.

Originally, the analysis of the blood and tissues of a healthy human being and of its maternal milk, revealed the presence of twelve inorganic salts. Subsequent analysis added many more such substances, but in microscopic amounts and they are known as "trace" elements, even though so they are essential for the life of the organism. Some of these apparently act as co-ordinators and others as activators of secondary chemical processes within the body.

All the substances of earth, sand and rock are weathered and washed down into the springs and rivers and many of the contents of the sea are carried in infinitesimally small amounts into the tissues of human beings through the food they eat. The microscopic amounts of these substances may be no more than a small part of an atom.

The eminent German physiological chemist, Bunge, has given this analysis of blood:[1]

In every 1,000 grams of blood cells:

Iron phosphate	0.998 gram
Potassium sulphate	0.132 gram
Potassium chloride	3.079 gram
Potassium phosphate	2.343 gram
Sodium phosphate	0.633 gram
Calcium phosphate	0.094 gram
Magnesium phosphate	0.060 gram

And in every 1,000 grams of the intercellular fluid:

Sodium chloride	5.545 gram

And with even smaller amounts of other salts.

Any imbalance of these salts or any disturbance in metabolism can cause disease and the needed dosage of a biochemic nutrient to meet the condition has to be reckoned accordingly in microscopic amounts. This is achieved by the trituration process in the preparation of these nutrient remedies.

These tissue salts in their natural state consist of closely packed particles of the elements and are thus not assimilable by the cell tissue. They are therefore "triturated", which is a crushing, and spreading-out process, by which the particles of the salt are mixed with pure sugar of milk, which is a convenient neutral medium in itself. The result is, an attenuation of the particle of the salt according to the number of times of spread and mixing.

The salts are prepared for medication in $3X^2$, 6X and 12X potency. Higher potencies of 30X and 200X are obtainable, they are also available in the mixed range of 3X-200X in each tissue salts. This is a combination of the various potencies scientifically prepared by high-powered machines in order to achieve a subdivision of the salt particles which correspond very closely to its counterpart in the living tissue.

It is best to give doses of the smallest suitable strength. By this means other functions of the cells which are proceeding normally will not be disturbed or any imbalance is not caused. In chronic condition of disease, however, several functions of cell life are likely to become involved and those several conditions will then need attention and given suitable treatment. The higher the trituration, the more divided and finer is the substance. The condition of some tissue cells requires a very fine or high trituration before the weakened cell tissue can absorb it. Some conditions may also require certain nutrients in large amounts, and the food intake then needs adjustment and possibly some food supplements.

These mineral elements, being a part of the nutrition of the body, support the food intake; the food has to supply the body's organic needs.

Being constituents of cell life and intercellular processes, these mineral elements are important factors in effective elimination of waste and worn-out cell products and in the dispersal of congestions harmful to the health of the body.

The cells of body tissue have the power to attract the substances from the blood needed for their nutrition. In ill-health, this power may be weakened and consequently a high (fine) trituration of the remedy might be needed.

It is difficult to make an exact alignment when considering the mineral elements contained in food and the potency of triturations of the prepared mineral remedies. Those minerals, which are present in our food, are generally present in the form of compounds, forming the structure of cereals, vegetables, fruits, and dairy products, and the digestive process is the simplification of these structures into assimilable factors. In comparison, the preparation of the inorganic mineral substances as biochemic tissue remedies is one of division into minute assimilable portions of an element.

In particular, brain and nerve cells attract as their related cell-salts–*Kali-p.*, *Mag-p.*, *Nat-p.*, and *Ferr-p.* Similarly, muscle cells, with the addition of *Kali-m.* Connective and living cells, by which the tissues are covered and connected with other body tissues and are also protected and given strength, especially attract and require *Silicea.* Elastic tissue, which includes cartilage and again the muscle cells, *Calc-f.* The cells of mucous membranes attract *Nat-m.* Bone tissue has an affinity for *Calc-f.*, *Calc-p.*, and *Mag-p.*, the skin attracts *Kali-s.* and *Silicea*; the hair cells also attract the same. *Ferr-p.* is needed by every cell of the body.

In addition, all conditions of first stage inflammations, raised temperature, soreness of throat, rash require *Ferr-p.* to assist the extra demand on the blood cells for hemoglobin and oxygen.

In chronic diseases, the most obvious symptom indicates the first requirement; the secondary and the general condition of the patient, most probably requires a supporting prescription for the constitutional imbalance or the basic tissue remedy may need supporting trace elements. Suitable doses of biochemic tissue remedies can provide all these requirements of the cells and intercellular tissues.

The number of cells constituting the dose is shown by the laboratory or the practitioner supplying these mineral remedies.

Age is bound to be a factor in recovery from illness or injury and from disease. It has been said that where a child takes a week to reinstate its health, an elderly person will need four or five times as long. But one does not need to wait for full recovery to enjoy a measure of relief and greater ease.

The therapeutic section outlines the treatments to be followed in various conditions of pain and disease, having the broad principles of cause and effect in mind. It has to be remembered, also, when diagnosing the condition, that it is the person or child, we wish to heal and not merely the symptom. Thus, a child with chronic eczema may first need a tonic for the pituitary gland or the nervous system before the skin condition will respond to the tissue remedies–*Kali-s.*, *Ferr-p.* and *Kali- m.* Consequently, this child and some of the chronic sufferers may need more experienced biochemic treatment than is contained within these Twelve Salts. Reference to these special requirements is also given in the therapeutic treatments. In short, for the diagnosis to be successful, one needs to be intuitive besides having the necessary physiological knowledge.

REFERENCES :

1. Ref: *Guide to Biochemic Treatment,* By C. Stirling Saunder, L. R. C. P. (Lond.).

2. And are now obtainable in any potency from IX upwards.

CHAPTER 2

The Twelve Inorganic Tissue Salts

	Therapeutic Name	Abbreviation
Fluoride of Lime (Calcarea fluorica)	Calc. fluor.	Calc-f.
Phosphate of Lime (Calcarea phosphorica)	Calc. phos.	Calc-p.
Sulphate of Lime (Calcarea sulphurica)	Calc. sulph.	Calc-s.
Phosphate of Iron (Ferrum phosphoricum)	Ferr. phos.	Ferr-p.
Chloride of Potash (Kalium muriaticum)	Kali. mur.	Kali-m.
Phosphate of Potash (Kalium phosphoricum)	Kali. phos.	Kali-p.
Phosphate of Magnesia (Magnesium phosphoricum)	Mag. phos.	Mag-p.
Chloride of Soda (Natrium muriaticum)	Nat. mur.	Nat-m.

Phosphate of Soda
(Natrium phosphoricum)   Nat. phos.   Nat-p.

Sulphate of Soda
(Natrium sulphuricum)   Nat. sulph.   Nat-s.

Silicic Acid
(Silicea)   Silicea   Sil.

CHAPTER 3

Functions of the Twelve Tissue Salts in the Healthy Human Body and the Potency and Dose Needed in Pain and Disease

So fundamental, so essentially necessary are the Tissue Salts in daily life that there follows a detailed discription of each and its uses, each under its special heading. Also shown are the *diseases and pain* resulting from an imbalance or deficiency of these Tissue Salts in the human body and suggested *doses and potencies* to be taken for relief and the restoration of health.

FLUORIDE OF LIME (CALCAREA FLUORICA)

This salt is a constituent of all the elastic fibres and epidermis. Elastic fibres are found in the skin, connective tissue and vascular walls. These tissue cells cover all organs, and form unbroken connections between the various tissues and organs. The surface of bones contains this salt and it forms the enamel of teeth.

Where there is an imbalance of this salt in the elastic fibres, organs are likely to prolapse and veins varicose. Flabbiness, generally shown in the flesh and in a hanging abdomen (pendulous abdomen) indicates a disturbance in the correct assimilation of this mineral from the food. This may similarly affect the heart muscle, which then suffers from dilatation. And the answer is to give a higher (finer) potency of the mineral to effect permeability of the tissue cells and so ensure correct assimilation. When the elastic fibres of blood vessels suffer a disturbance of the molecules of Calcarea fluorica, pathological enlargements of blood vessels take place, presenting as, hemorrhoidal tumors, varices, enlarged veins and vascular tumors. Loss of this salt in the system presents as:

i. Hard, knotty exudation on the surface of a bone.

ii. Relaxation of elastic fibres causes dilatation of vessels, relaxation and displacement of uterus, relaxation of abdominal wall, hemorrhage from womb, absence of after-pains.

iii. Exudation of keratin from the epidermal cells.

Cataract, tumors of the eyelids. Corneal ulcers, if edges are hard. Calcareous deposits on the tympani. Tinnitus. Adenoidal growths; hypertrophy of Luschka's tonsil. *The chief remedy in true croup.*

Rough and sensitive teeth indicate a poor distribution of this mineral in the body or an actual deficiency, and it is probably the reason for a late dentition in an infant. Enamel of teeth becomes rough and deficient. Teeth become loose in their sockets.

If muscle and tendons suffer a strain or if they lose their firm shape and form a tumor or lymphatic glands become enlarged, if carbuncles form, or hard ulcers appear in the primary state before any inflammation or suppuration has commenced, then these are indications of an imbalance in the particles of this mineral salt, which requires the use of suitable doses of *Calc-f.* as a remedy. And if the skin runs into cuts and cracks with crust formation, this condition too, indicates a need for *Calc-f.*

Some cases of gastric vomiting probably require *Calc-f.* for an imbalance of this mineral localized in the gastric connective tissue. If, however, the vomit is greenish, *Nat-s.* will be needed, or *Nat-p.* if the vomit is frothy and sour smelling. (See reference to these two salts.) Again, where the urine is pungent, due to a similar localized disturbance, and if the urine is an apparently healthy elimination, doses of *Calc-f.* will give the relief.

For ruptures, hemorrhoids and hemorrhage of the uterus, again because of a local weakness of the connective walls, take doses of this remedy. These conditions will most likely require a combination of several tissue salts in alternation, e.g., if bleeding hemorrhoids are the conditions, *Ferr-p.* will be needed in alternation with *Calc-f.* In weakness of the throat where the larynx is relaxed, *Calc-f.* is again the indicated tissue salt, in alternation with, most probably, *Kali-m.*

Indurated cervical glands of stony hardness. Small goitres.

Chronic conditions of synovitis need *Calc-f.* to correct the imbalance in the affected tissues, and also for any swelling of the covering of bones. Exostosis on fingers. Osseous growths and enlargement of bones, with or without caries, especially of traumatic origin. *Felon* (3X trituration).

Aneurysm, at an early stage may be reduced or kept in check by *Calc-f.* and *Ferr-p.*, provided iodide of potash has not been taken. It is the *chief remedy to restore the contractivity of the elastic fibres in blood vessels.* Dilatation of the heart with palpitation. *Chief remedy for vascular tumors with dilated blood vessels.* Varicose ulceration of the veins.

Displacements of the uterus. Tones up the contractile power of the uterus in cases of flooding. Huntarian chancre, for the induration.

Skin is hard and thickened, tendency to fissure formation. *Fissures or cracks of the palms.* Keratosis.

In the tissues, its deficiency causes solid infilterations. *Indurated glands of stony hardness. Knots, kernals and tumors in female breast.*

Doses of this tissue salt is a remedy for obesity in alternation with doses of *Calc-p.* to adjust poor assimilation of starch and fats in the meals. At the same time, the intake of these food items needs to be checked.

When using this tissue salt for acute conditions, give *Calc-f.* in 6X potency, and if the symptoms are severe, a dose every ten or fifteen minutes is indicated. As soon as the condition is easier, the doses should be taken less frequently and then at two-hourly or three-hourly intervals. Chronic conditions generally do better if higher potencies are used. Should a chronic condition flare up, a high potency of the salt taken at half-hourly intervals will be needed for a short time. As soon as there is an abatement, the doses can be reduced to four times a day or even once a day if the case is advanced or the patient is an elderly.

Very young children are best given a half-dose every ten minutes in acute conditions.

If the combination potency 3-200X is used, it is equally suitable for acute and chronic conditions, additional frequency only being needed for acute conditions.

Higher potencies give best results, especially in bone affections.

Can be used externally in anal fissure, bony growths, hemorrhoids, varicose veins and whitlow. For application, dissolve

20 grains of the desired potency is 1/2 a glass of water and apply it on cotton, lint, etc.

PHOSPHATE OF LIME (CALCAREA PHOSPHORICA)

Farmers and gardeners are known to this salt. It is a main constituent of many of the productive soils.

This salt is also a main constituent of all the cells of the body and the body fluids. It is found in blood plasma and corpuscles, saliva, gastric juice, bones, connective tissues, teeth, milk, etc. It has a special chemical affinity for albumen and is required wherever albumen or albuminous substances are found in secretions.

This tissue salt promotes proper growth and nutrition in children. It is a nutritive salt for the periosteum and for bones. It is of greatest importance for cell growth. Also, it supplies new blood cells, becoming the first remedy in anemia and chlorosis. Without it there is no coagulation and spasms and pains caused by anemia. The sphere of action includes all bone diseases. It is of great value in rickets in combination with specific foods and vitamins.

Another important feature is its restorative power after acute diseases, either directly or preparing the way for other remedies by stimulating the system to their action. Hence, it is an important *intercurrent remedy.*

Calc-p. can be used with advantage in all cases of debility and in convalescence, for tuberculous condition and particularly where there is poor assimilation of food and consequent defective · nutrition. It has proved to be a real tonic is chronic wasting diseases; anemia of young, rapidly growing people, in women weakened by rapid child bearing, prolonged suckling or excessive menses or leucorrhea (like the white of an egg).

In cases where discharges have lowered and exhausted the system, this remedy should follow doses of *Calc-s.*, which will arrest them.

There is general lack of vital heat and *aggravation from change of weather and from wet weather. Sensitive to cold.*

If broken bones do not unite or are slow to do so or the *fontanelles in children remain open* too long, use *Calc-p.* as a remedy. Skull is soft and thin. Chronic hydrocephalus. Spinal curvature. Rheumatism of joints with coldness or numbness; *sensation as if parts were asleep.*

In dental caries (*Fl-ac., mag-p., sil.*)

Polyp-nasal, rectal and uterine. Freckles are lessened by the use of this remedy. Pains where bones form sutures or symphyses.

In old age, where the regenerative functions decrease in the nervous tissue. Senile cutaneous and vaginal itching.

Flabby, shrunken, emaciated children having a waxy complexion. Rickets. Of use during dentition, convulsions and spasms; abdominal colic with green, slimy, hot, offensive, noisy, sputtering diarrhoea. Cholera infantum. Slow in learning to walk and delayed dentition. Rapid decay of teeth.

This salt is needed as a remedy in conditions of the blood and circulation, like anemia which result in cramps or spasms with numbness (not to be confused with spasm of the nerves with shooting pains which needs a different tissue remedy, *Mag-p.*). If hands and feet are always cold or if the hands and feet are ice-like and clammy or if the circulation is slow or retarded, making parts of the body feel as if they were asleep, *Calc-p.* is the indicated remedy.

Tip of nose icy cold. Chronic colds in anemic and scrofulous patients. *Involuntary sighing.*

This remedy is needed in diphtheria if the larynx is involved, and in croup (in alternation with *Kali-s.* to hasten the expulsion of dead cell material). Sore aching in throat; pain in every direction on swallowing. *Chronic enlargement of tonsils.*

Calc-p. should be used in a high potency by those who catch cold easily and who are very subject to catarrh; one dose a day should generally be sufficient to cure this liability. In these cases it may be necessary to adjust the balance of the general diet.

If there is a tendency to form "stones" of phosphates - the diagnosis may be given as calculi - doses of a high potency of this salt would correct the mineral imbalance present in this condition, and should be used from time to time to prevent a recurrence. Enuresis in old people and small children with great debility.

Some cases of obesity need this remedy in conjunction with *Calc-f.* and possibly some small adjustment in the food intake, particularly as to the consumption of starch.

Conditions of hydrocele, orchitis, sore breast in women, uterine displacement and chronic ovaritis are also indications of a disturbance or deficiency of phosphate of lime, and *Calc-p.*, is the indicated tissue salt. The general food habits may also need supplementing.

Night sweats, especially is phthisis indicate a disturbance in metabolism which this remedy is likely to adjust; and some cases of epilepsy will be helped by doses of this tissue salt.

In cases of considerable flatulence, if doses of *Mag-p.* (in hot water) are insufficient to cure the condition, follow up the dose of *Mag-p.* with a dose of *Calc-p.*, and repeat this procedure after each meal or at stated intervals while the attack persists. Craves indigestible things like bacon, ham, salted or smoked meats. Abdomen sunken and flabby, useful in summer complaints, marasmus and teething children. Abdominal hernia. *Fistula in ano alternating with chest symptoms.*

When giving this remedy for gastric trouble, as a restorative after debilitating diseases, and usually when there is anemia, cellules of *Nat-m.* may need to be given also to assist assimilation of calcium (see *Nat-m.*)

All conditions needing this nutrient remedy can be given the 6X (or 3-200X) except in tumors, which will require a higher potency, the 12X (or 3-200X) is advised which is likely to be effective. 3X-6X are usually employed, giving most satisfactory results, though 30-200 potency have given brilliant clinical results.

Calcarea carbonica	Calcarea phosphorica
Acts best in light haired and blue eyed people.	Adapted to dark complexion, dark eyes and hair.

Calc-p. occupies a ground between *Calc.* and *Phos.*

SULPHATE OF LIME (CALCAREA SULPHURICA)

This salt is known in the commercial market as *plaster of Paris* and its surgical use is as plaster casts for the support of fractured limbs.

In the human body it is a constituent, in the form of minute particles, of all connective tissue and is contained also in the liver cells.

This salt in the physical tissues attracts water to itself and in that way hastens the destruction of certain worn-out cells. In the liver, its presence effects the destruction of red blood cells which have finished their life cycle and have arrived at the liver as partially waste products. If, then, there are insufficient particles of *Calc-s.* in the liver, the blood becomes overcharged with these worn-out cells and skin eruptions generally result.

If the deficiency of this salt extends to the connective tissues, the skin eruptions are likely to become deep abscesses or chronically oozing ulcers. It is indicated where varicose ulcers have become chronic and sanious - causing much lowering and draining of the system. Again, if the face is covered with pimples and pustules which continue to suppurate, *Calc-s.* is the tissue remedy.

This remedy is used for third stage inflammations (exudations of pus) as it stands in close relation to suppurations, particularly where wateriness of the tissues is also present; the pus itself may be watery, as in some conditions of bronchitis.

Cures purulent discharge from mucous membranes and purulent exudations in serous sacs; also cures tubercular ulcers or abscesses of intestines. *Presence of pus with a vent is the general indication for this drug.*

This nutrient remedy can be useful after doses of *Nat-s.* in kidney diseases.

Scald head of children; crusta lactea, with purulent discharge. Much dandruff. Frontal headaches with sickness are probably due to a general deficiency of *Calc-s* in the connective tissues of the nerves; if the *elderly* have neuralgia, it may be from the same cause; and where there is an extreme touchiness of the nerves with much sensitiveness, *Calc-s.* is again the remedy.

Indicated in deep seated abscess of cornea, hypopyon; after *Silicea.*

Colds; yellow, purulent secretions. Suppurating sore throat. Quinsy.

Gum boils.

Diarrhoea, dysentery purulent. Painless abscess about the anus in cases of fistula.

Chronic cystitis with pus formation; nephritis, give alternativly with *Silicea*. Gonorrhea; chronic suppurating stage of syphilis.

Empyema; pneumonia—third stage.

Burning and itching of soles and feet. Herpetic eruptions. Boils, cuts, wounds, burns, scalds, carbuncles, chilblains, pimples, small pox, ulcers, etc. all in suppurating stage. If *Calc-s.* is given after *Sil.,* it will cause the abscess to heel.

Suggested Doses: For a chronic condition – A dose of 6X or of 3-200X, three times a day; for elderly people – A dose of 12X or of 3-200X, three times a day, but if the condition is long standing, this dose only twice a day; for young people – Give a dose of 6X or 3-200X, four times or even six times a day where the condition is probably more of an acute nature.

Note: In the last years of his life, Dr. Schüssler discarded *Calc-s.* from his list, leaving only *eleven*, instead of twelve tissue remedies.

Calc-s. resembles *Hepar,* but acts deeper and more intensely, and is often useful after *Hepar* has ceased to act.

PHOSPHATE OF IRON (FERRUM PHOSPHORICUM)

Iron is present not only in the hemoglobin of blood cells but in all the cells of the body, except those of nerves. These, however, are lined with protective connective tissues, containing blood (with its iron), which penetrates between the cells and nourishes them; phosphate of iron is found in hair cells and in the muscular membranes of the blood and lymph vessels.

Hemoglobin of blood is composed of iron in combination with the protein, globin. Its presence in the tissues is the means by which carbon dioxide in those tissues is given off and returned to the lungs. Iron in association with *Kali-s.* which carries oxygen to all tissues of the body. The presence of iron in the tissues also activates various processes in the body, including that of releasing energy from the food that has been digested.

The red corpuscles in the blood have their cycle of life, comprising from two to six weeks, and on their disintegration the iron from them is stored in the liver until it is used again. Healthy kidneys hold back much of the iron that would be otherwise lost in the urine, though some part of the body's iron content is lost in the process of sloughing of skin, perspiration and through feces.

Copper is an essential element in catalysing (activating) the manufacture of hemoglobin in the body. Thus, the body not only requires iron, but also the trace element, copper to co-operate with it.

The body only absorbs iron when it requires, but it is one of the first requirements for health and adequate supply should be present in the daily food. Iron that is not wanted and has not been absorbed from the food is duly excreted as fecal waste.

Insufficient hydrochloric acid in the digestive juices may prevent the absorption of iron even from those foods which contain it in an easily assimilable form. This can be a reason for iron deficiency in the blood even though the intake of suitable food may be adequate.

If there is an imbalance in the particles of iron in the muscular fibres, they become relaxed. If this occurs in muscular coats of vessels, there is dilatation and congestion, which may in turn lead to increased blood pressure, wall rupture and finally hemorrhage. If, then, such a condition does not adjust itself, inflammation of various tissues results. Most physical illness commences in this manner, and if used promptly, doses of this nutrient will most probably heal the conditon. If, however, a further stage of inflammation has been reached (second and third stage inflammation), giving exudations and secretions, prescribe this tissue remedy in alternation with that indicated by the type of exudation.

One cause of continous diarrhoea is the relaxed walls of the intestinal *villi*; a cause of constipation is a weak bowel action consequent upon relaxed muscular walls of the *intestines*. In both conditions it is probable that insufficient iron is being absorbed from the food, either from inadequate supplies or from too little hydrochloric acid in the digestive juices. In both these cases, doses of this tissue salt can be expected to bring the condition to normal if they are also alternated with similar doses of *Nat-m.* in a little water to correct the digestive juices. If costive, the stools are dry, which is an indication of trouble, and the remedy. The daily meals should, of course, be checked to see that adequate supplies of *assimilable* iron are, in fact, being taken.

Through its power of attracting oxygen, iron becomes a useful remedy in diseases of the blood cells like anemia, chlorosis and leukemia.

Ferr-p. is the biochemic remedy for:

i.   First stage of all inflammations. It improves the quality of blood to fight the illness better. This tissue remedy should be used at the commencement of all colds, sore throat and influenza, for the first stages of all fevers, for all children's fevers – scarlet fever, whooping cough, measles – for the first stage and also during the illness, and for similar conditions in adults; also for the first stage of bronchitis, pleurisy and rheumatism, and as one of the remedies in neuritis at the commencement of pain.

ii. Pain worse motion, better from cold.

iii. Hemorrhages caused by hyperemesis.

iv. Fresh wounds caused by mechanical injuries.

Hyperemia, of the brain producing delirium, maniacal mood. Dizziness from congestion, consequence of anger.

Congestive headaches probably need this remedy (with, in addition, doses of *Kali-s.*), as also some cases of insomnia from lack of iron nutrition to the brain. If, after some hours of concentrated brainwork in the late evening, sleep is elusive, a dose of this remedy followed ten minutes later by a similar dose of *Kali-p.* can clear the brain and natural sleep should follow shortly after.

Headache, especially of children with throbbing sensation, *red face* and suffused eyes. Florid complexion.

Eyes inflamed, red, burning; retinal congestion. *Sensation as if grains of sand were under the eyelids.*

First stage otitis, pain paroxysmal and radiating in character; tinnitus. First stage of all colds. Predisposition to catch cold. Smarting especially in right nasal passage, worse inspiration. *Epistaxis.*

Ulcerated, sore throat; red inflamed with much pain. First stage of diphtheria. *Bronchitis of children;* congestion of lungs, hemoptysis; loss of voice; *hoarseness. Acute, febrile or initiatory stage of all inflammatory affections of the respiratory tract.*

First stage of gastritis. Vomiting of indigested food; *of bright red blood.* Inflamed and incarcerated hernia.

Hematuria; first stage cystitis with heat, pain and fever. *Incontinence of urine from weakness of sphincter.*

Also, first stage orchitis, epididymitis, gonorrhea and mastitis. Congestive dysmenorrhea.

Congestive stage of carditis, pericarditis, endocarditis and arteritis. In aneurysm to establish normal circulation and remove complications arising from excessive action of the heart. Varicose veins.

Hyperemia of the skin. Abscess, boils, carbuncles and felons – at the commencement of these affections *Ferr-p.* reduces the heat, congestion, pain and throbbing of great value.

The severe pain from inflamed piles is quickly relieved with this remedy; use it also if they are bleeding. In these cases a dose every ten minutes is advised until the most acute condition has lessened, then every hour, and then two-hourly intervals are suggested. The condition can be treated externally as well, using a lotion of this tissue salt, some three doses to half a cupful of warm water.

Acts brilliantly in old people. Is also an excellent general remedy for children, in alternation with *Calc-p.* and particularly if they are listless, have no appetite or have teething fever. A 12X potency of *Ferr-p.* and a 6X potency of *Calc-p.* is suggested or both in the 3–200X potency, three doses of each daily until recovery, which will generally be accomplished in twenty-four hours.

The simplest indications for the use of this tissue remedy is a rising temperature. The head is hot, with internal shivering, brilliant and inflamed eyes, and if any part of the body is obviously hot and inflamed or if the throat is sore. All catarrhal and inflammatory fevers during the chill or initial stage; rigors, heat, quick pulse and pain.

For all recent physical injuries to assist healing of the parts in supplying the needed additional iron particles. Doses should be taken internally at ten-minute intervals and externally as a lotion with a bandage by dissolving three doses in half a cupful of warm water.

If the trouble is *highly acute,* take dose every ten minutes, but half-hourly doses would generally be considered suitable for acute conditions, and then hourly and less frequently as the condition eases.

Many illnesses advance to second stage inflammation, either because they have not been observed and dealt with in time or the patient's general constitution has allowed inroad of the diseases to a further stage. The use of *Ferr-p.* will always assist in breaking down the diseases and in fortifying the life of the body. When the condition has advanced to second and third stage inflammations, the indicated tissue remedies for those conditions should first be given; *Ferr-p.* is also given as a second or third requirement, and less frequently than the main remedy.

In very debilitated or elderly people, higher potencies of *Ferr-p.* are likely to be more suitable; a 12X, 30X or even 200X can be used. These can be taken for acute and chronic conditions; doses might well be taken hourly for acute conditions, and twice or three times a day where the trouble is more of a chronic nature.

For most adults, unless in a weak state of health, the 3X potency is suitable for most acute conditons, and a 12X potency would probably be required, if the trouble has become chronic over a period of time.

The 3-200X potency cover most requirements, the frequency of the dose being the only adjustment for the acute and chronic conditions, and the slower metabolism of the elderly needing one or two doses a day for long-standing conditions. It stands midway between *Acon.* and *Gels.*

CHLORIDE OF POTASH (KALIUM MURIATICUM)

Potassium chloride has an attraction in the body for fibrin – a nitrogenous protein, causing fibrinous exudations. *Kali-m.* is found in blood corpuscles, muscles, nerve and brain cells, and intercellular fluids.

If there is tissue irritation under the surface of cells of the skin, these cells increase their natural activity of excreting cell substances and the skin is raised into a blister. In the body *Kali-m.* unites with hydrogen and forms hydrochloric acid. This then dissolves the excrete. This happens in smallpox, chickenpox, scarlet fever and measles. *Kali-m.* is indicated as a remedy when the activity of excretion has commenced, that is, after the fever has begun to abate. In the first stage of fever, *Ferr-p.* is needed.

The lining cells of all body tissues form a thin covering membrane. These secrete sufficient fluid to nourish the adjacent tissues and keep them moist. If these membranes get inflamed, the secreting activity of these cells increases. The secretions will at first be watery and copious, and need *Nat-m.* If the inflammation extended to the second stage, *Kali-m.* is needed and suitable doses will dissolve the fibrinous element in these secretions. They are generally recognized as a greyish-white catarrh. Doses of *Kali-m.* will clear this catarrh by adjusting the secreting activity.

This salt corresponds to the second stage of inflammation of serous membranes, when the exudation is of a plastic or fibrinous character. *Kali-m.* answers croupous and diphtheric exudations.

Fibrinous exudations in the interstitial connective tissues; lymphatic enlargements, infiltrated inflammations, cutaneous eruptions from bad vaccine, virus, etc. The principal general characteristic symptoms are a white or grey coating at the base of the tongue, white or grey exudations and discharges or expectoration of a thick, white, fibrinous character.

Congestions and inflammations, second stage of any organ or part of body.

Eczema will be resolved by this remedy, if it is in the secondary stage of inflammation, that is, if the skin is blistering and commencing to excrete, but all pathological skin conditions are invariably benefited by *Kali-s*. Absesses, boils, carbuncles, in the second stage. Crusta lactea. Chilblains.

Croupous conditions, pneumonia and pleurisy (with plastic exudations and adhesions), indicate a need for this remedy. Also bronchial asthma, second stage of bronchitis when thick, white phlegm forms, wheezing, rales or rattling sound of air passing through thick, tenacious mucus in the bronchi.

Generally the sole remedy required in most cases of diphtheria. Tonsils inflamed, enlarged so much, can hardly breathe. Grey patches or spots in throat. White deposits. Can gargle with this salt also.

This secondary inflammation is present in mumps, with consequent swelling of the glands, and in some cases of deafness where the eustachian tube becomes swollen and congested, and doses of this tissue remedy can be expected to clear it. Some cases of chronic catarrhal deafness need a high potency to be effective. *Chronic catarrhal conditions of the middle ear.* Excessive granulations. Moist exfoliation of epithelial layer of tympanic membrane. *Snapping* and noises in the ears.

For retinal exudation and granulation of the eyelids, and where there is dry granular inflammation from the nose, *Kali-m.* is the indicated tissue remedy.

If menses are painful and membranous – bringing shreds of thin, dead tissue, use this tissue salt in alternation with *Mag-p*. If the menstrual blood is dark and clotted, this is a certain indication for the need of this tissue salt, as well as for leucorrhea, the whitish, thick, non-irritating exudation from the vagina. Chief remedy in chronic cystitis, with discharge of thick, white mucus. Second stage gonorrhea and orchitis.

Kali-m. in suitable potencies is indicated where the liver is sluggish, with constipation giving only light, greyish stools; for piles with dark clotted blood; second stage of peritonitis, typhlitis and peri-typhlitis and for rheumatic fever after the high temperature has abated, and for which *Ferr-p.* would be needed.

For typhoid, enteric and typhus fevers, this remedy is indicated with *Kali-p.*

Again, *Kali-m.* is indicated in mucus colitis; the earlier stage of inflammation and pain requires *Ferr-p.* Diarrhoea after fatty foods.

Warts on the hands are healed with this tissue remedy and it is also indicated in shingles and acne.

If given immediately, the 3X potency as a lotion will control the blistering in burns and scalds. (*Ferr-p.* also, in alternation, it should relieve the pain.)

Dull aching pains in any part of the body needs this remedy; the condition is to be treated as an acute one, requiring 3X potency (or 3-200X potency), a dose every twenty minutes.

If starch and fatty foods are taken with difficulty, this is most probably due to a deficiency of *Kali-m.* in the saliva, where it is an aid for the effective digestion of starch, and one dose each morning in the 6X potency is advised as a constitutional remedy.

This tissue salt is also indicated for jaundice when the condition arises due to a chill, because of catarrh of the duodenum, and for asthma when this is due to gastric disorder, as the condition requires *Kali-m.* to assist secretion of hydrochloric acid. For this reason it is an important remedy in epilepsy, especially if occuring with or after suppression of eczema or other eruptions. Disease of the heart, liver or kidneys, *with dropsy*, may also require suitable doses of this salt.

In all acute conditions, the 6X potency of this tissue salt can be expected to give the correct results, taken internally, a dose every twenty minutes; where it is needed externally as a lotion, the 3X potency is preferable. In chronic conditions of sluggishness of the liver with constipation, a 12X potency is advised, a dose three times a day.

The 3-200X potency is suitable for all cases; a dose every twenty minutes for acute conditions, and three times a day where the condition is chronic.

Three doses in half a cupful of water makes a suitable lotion, applied on lint.

In general, it is a *sluggish* remedy for *sluggish* symptoms and *sluggish* constitutions being anti-scrofulous, anti-sycotic and anti-syphilitic.

SULPHATE OF POTASH (KALIUM SULPHURICUM)

This tissue salt has a special relationship with cells forming the lining of the skin and those which form the internal mucous lining of all the organs of the body.

If the balance of this salt is disturbed in these tissues, there is a disruption in these lining cells and an exudation of yellowish, slimy matter results. Papules of the skin secreting this type of exudation, usually with irritation, indicate this imbalance in the surface cells; and a yellow coating at the back of the tongue is a symptoms of this condition involving the inner membrane of the digestive tract.

This tissue salt shares with *Ferr-p.* the activity of carrying oxygen to all tissues of the body.

Kali-s. in conjunction with the oxygen in the body activates the destruction of its worn-out cells and at the same time it prevents undue dissolution. It is a third-stage inflammation tissue remedy, needed for its action in normalizing such processes. Epidermis and epithelial cells poorly fed with oxygen loosen and desquamate easily. If oxygen is brough to the suffering part by

Kali-s., formation of new cells is furthered, and these hasten, by their activity, to promote desquamation of old ones.

Kali-s., then, is the tissue remedy in third stage inflammatory conditions of bronchitis, whooping cough, penumonia, when the exudations are of yellowish, slimy nature; and in *ail* catarrhs having this type of exudation, whichever part of the body is involved – in gastric, intestinal, laryngeal, nasal or aural catarrhs; and in all those diseases when peeling conditions of the skin are in process.

Rise in temperature at night producing an evening aggravation. It assists in promoting perspiration.

A grand characteristic of this salt is *evening aggravation* and amelioration in cold, open air. Diseases caused by retrocession of eruptions.

By reason of its relationship with oxygen in the physical tissues, this is the tissue salt to be used in all those conditions – whether it be asthma, rheumatism or gastric fever which are worse in hot rooms and in hot atmospheres or when the fever rises appreciably at night and is near normal in the mornings.

In case of insufficiency of this tissue salt, the physical tissues suffer from a need of oxygen. This is experienced in alternate hot and cold feelings, in weariness and heaviness, in vague feelings of anxiety or sadness, in heavy headaches or as pains in the limbs which are of an indefinite nature and tend to move about, and in rheumatism or neuralgia where these pains move from one part to another part of the body. These symptoms worsen in the evening and are relieved by cold, fresh air. Scaly eruptions mostly on arms, better from hot weather.

Kali-s. is indicated in bronchial asthma when the condition is accentuated by being in warm rooms or during hot weather. Yellow expectoration. Pneumonia; coarse rales; rattling in chest.

This remedy is needed in conditions of peritonitis with the tympanitic abdomen; in jaundice, if the tongue has a yellowish coating implying a third stage catarrh as its cause; and in colic if this is catarrhal and has not responded to treatment with *Mag-p.*

Indigestion which gives a feeling of fullness at the base of the stomach may also be catarrhal, in which case the tongue will almost certainly show it, but the condition indicates an insufficiency of the particles of this salt needed for effective oxidation in the tissues involved. Yellow, slimy, watery, purulent diarrhoea with characteristic tongue. *Violent itching of anus.*

All third stage inflammations producing tissue degenerations of the surface cells of the mouth, tongue, lips, indicate a need for this tissue salt, and any part of the skin or internal membrane affected in this manner, as in psoriasis, eczema in its third stage and in dandruff; nasal obstructions with ulceration. Colds with yellow, slimy expectoration; smell lost, ozena. Fetid discharges of the ear indicate a similar involvement. Stinking otorrhea.

Yellow crusts on eyelids; yellow or greenish purulent discharge from the eyes.

Skin lesions are vesico-pustular and papular. Greenish-yellow exudate with formation of a thin crust which is loosely attached. Copious scaling of scalp, which is moist and sticky.

Pulsations all over the body. Gonorrhea, leucorrhea – slimy, yellow.

All these catarrhal conditions, bronchitis, jaundice and established skin conditions are likely to be of a chronic nature and treatment with 6X potency (or 3-200X potency), a dose three times a day, should quickly improve the condition. A similar potency and number of doses is likely to be correct for conditions of dandruff and a lotion of some three doses of the 3X potency in half a cup of warm water should be additionally effective.

Vaginal discharges having the yellowish exudation are a chronic condition, catarrhal in nature, and doses of 6X (or 3-200X) potency, three times a day should quickly effect healing, provided other health measures are adequate.

Heavy headaches, indigestion, neuralgia, feelings of alternate shivering and suffocation, difficult or absent menses are all indications of this drug. These conditions when recurring are of a transitory nature and are treated as acute conditions. A dose of 3X potency (or 3-200X) is correct in these cases, given frequently, every ten minutes, every twenty minutes, and then hourly, if further treatment is required. As soon as relief is felt, showing the tissues are reacting to the tissue remedy, the doses should be taken less and less frequently. This is a certain rule for acute conditions. In chronic conditions when there is an *alteration* in the symptoms presented, showing a partial clearance of the trouble, a change of tissue remedy is indicated.

POTASSIUM PHOSPHATE (KALIUM PHOSPHORICUM)

Potassium phosphate is an important mineral constituent of all animal fluids and tissues, notably of brain, nerves, muscles and blood cells. It is, in fact, found in all tissues of the body, and is hence, indispensible to the formation of tissues. It is antiseptic in character and counteracts decay in the organism, giving the physical tissues vitality. Adynamia and decay are characteristic states of *Kali-p.*

A disturbance in *Kali-p.* molecules presents as:

i. *In mental sphere:* Bashfulness, anxiety, fear, tearfulness, Suspicious, homesickness, weakness of memory, depression, etc.

ii. *In vasomotor nerves:* Pulse first small and frequent, later retardation.

iii. *In sensory nerves:* Pain with paralytic sensation.

iv. *In motor nerves:* Weakness of nerve response and corresponding weak muscle to paralysis.

v. *Trophic fibres of sympathetic nerves:* Retardation or complete cessation of nutrition to the fibres causing softening and degeneration of the involved nerves.

Conditions arising from want of nerve power like, prostration, excretion, loss of mental vigor, depression, etc. *Prostration of mind, nerves and muscles. Neurasthenia* muscular debility after acute diseases. Atrophic condition in old people.

Kali-p. is an essential element in the processes of metabolism and in the assimilation of digested fats. It is also essential for the process of effectual respiration within the tissues.

In all putrefactive conditions within the body, this tissue salt is needed as a remedy. It is indicated in appendicitis due to a putrefactive bowel. It is the chief remedy in septic conditions, in offensive secretions and diarrhoeas, in septic hemorrhages and in gangrene.

Kali-p. is the chief remedy for typhoid and typhus fevers, and in enteric fever. In these conditions alternating doses of *Kali-m.* are needed to support the action of *Kali-p.* In stomatitis and in albuminuria due to faulty metabolism—*Kali-p.* is again the suitable tissue salt. Brain fag from over–work. Loss of memory, general irritability. Hysteria from sudden emotions. Cerebral anemia. Gangrenous conditions.

This tissue remedy is especially indicated for all pathological excited states, as in melancholia and obsessional fears; also for sleep walking. It is given for concussion of the brain and in delirium; for loss of mental power and for prostration after great exertion resulting in muscular atrophy or producing spasms and cramps. Night terrors of children.

It is the tissue remedy for sleeplessness when it is due to excitement or brain fatigue from additional stimulation, either from pleasure or overwork. When insomnia becomes chronic, *Kali-p.* doses need the addition of the relative trace elements, all in suitable potencies. These are obtainable.

This tissue salt is needed for alopecia, nettle-rash and malignant pemphigus; for asthma, if it is purely nervous; for nervous palpitation, where the gastritis; gastric ulcer. A nervous, "all gone" sensation at the pit of stomach. Stomachache from fright or excitement. Diarrhoea painless, watery, from fright or depression with great prostration. *Noisy, offensive flatus.*

Atrophy, wasting diseases with putrid stools.

200X potency is advised.

Kali-p. is indicated to reduce fever and pulse if *Ferr-p.* has failed.

Where the menses are excessive, this tissue salt is needed in alternation with *Ferr-p.* It is also given for colic. Amenorrhea with depression of spirits, lassitude and general nervous debility. Leucorrhea yellowish, acrid. *Intense sexual desire.* Puerperal mania; childbed fever. Impotence in men.

Sciatica and neuritis indicate a need for this remedy in alternation with *Ferr-p.* Paroxysms of pain, followed by exhaustion. *Neuralgic pains,* in any organ with depression, failure of strength, sensitiveness to light and noise; better pleasant excitement, gentle motion; worst when quiet or alone. Paralytic or rheumatic lameness; better from gentle motion. Paralysis of any part of body; partial, paraplegia, hemiplegia; or of bladder, lids, etc; paralysis usually comes on suddenly. Locomotor paralysis. *Itching of palms and soles.* Burning of feet fidgety feeling in feet. Muscular weakness after severe illness.

Nervousness without reasonable cause. Makes "mountains out of molehills". Paroxysms of pain, followed by exhaustion. Neuralgic pains, in any organ with depression, failure of strength, sensitiveness to light and noise; better pleasant excitement, gentle motion; worse when quiet or alone.

If children become acutely fretful, *Kali-p.* is needed in alternation with *Nat-p.*

Fevers need to be treated as acute conditions to commence with. As soon as good reactions are established and the condition shows an improvement, the doses at twenty minute intervals will then be given much in less frequently and in alternation with a second or third remedy indicated by the stage of the disease.

If the putrefactive or septic conditions are not accompanied by *fever* they probably need to be treated as chronic diseases and a dose, three times a day is likely to be most suitable. The minimal dose may be difficult to give but it can be extraordinarily effective if correctly prescribed.

Diseases of the spinal nerves and motor nerves causing difficulty in the use of muscles and control of function are likely to be of a highly chronic nature, the disease having established itself some time before it has been diagnosed. These conditions need biochemic prescriptions incorporating trace elements in addition to *Kali-p.* without which this tissue salt is not likely to be fully operative. (People suffering from these conditions are likely to benefit from *gentle,* experienced massage and directed exercises, depending on the extent of the condition. These measures increase the nutriton of all the tissues and assist the circulation to carry away its retrograde fluids. Their daily meals need to provide them with sufficient vitamins.)

Alopecia, nettle-rash, malignant pemphigus and nervous asthma, once established, will require treatment like chronic conditions, and are given three doses daily of *Kali-p.* in 200X or preferably, 3-200X potency.

Worse excitement, worry, mental and physical exertion. *Cold air aggravates all pains,* when alone. Characteristic ameliorations are gentle motion, eating, under-excitement and company.

This salt works best in lower potencies.

All conditions which suddenly present themselves and appear to need this tissue remedy may be judged as acute, but on continuation of the condition, the nature of the trouble will have to be regarded as a chronic one and doses given only three or four times a day.

PHOSPHATE OF MAGNESIA (MAGNESIUM PHOSPHORICUM)

This mineral salt is another constituent of blood cells, bones and teeth, brain (more of grey substance) and nerves, and muscle cells. If its molecules are out of balance in these tissues, cramps and spasms result, and if this condition runs to inflammation, neuralgia or even paralysis may result. Here the action of *Mag-p.* is the reverse of that of iron. By functional disturbance of molecules of the latter, muscular fibres relax; through the functional disturbances of the magnesium molecules they contract.

Mag-p. is the chief tissue salt in effecting functional activity of the motor nerves. This tissue salt is therefore indicated in all pains with the exception of burning pains. Especially related to cramping pains. Indicated in sharp, shooting, constricting pains giving spasm. *Purely antispasmodic;* lightening-like pains accompanied by a constricting feeling; often changing locality. *Relieved by warmth, pressure and bending double. Worse on right side, from cold and touch.*

It is the indicated tissue remedy in tetanus and lockjaw (other than conditions of dislocation), functional cramps of writers and artists., Piano or violin players' cramps. Nocturnal neuralgias with spasmodic muscular contractions, spasms, lightening-like pains. *Chorea. Lauguid, tired, exhausted* and angina. Also for yawning and shivering if it is spasmodic. Cramps in calves, Sciatica.

Palpitations of the heart if it is spasmodic. The indications for this tissue remedy are spasms and shooting pains; those for *Kali-p.* are weakness and the inability to make a movement.

Headache; after mental labor; relieved by application of warmth, pressure and walking in open air. *Orbital and supra-orbital neuralgia,* worse right side.

Otalgia, of nervous character, worse behind right ear; worse cold air and washing face and neck with cold water. Prosopalgia.

Severe pain in decayed or filled teeth; toothache, better heat and hot liquids. Complaints of teething children; spasms, colic and flatulence.

Mag-p. is needed in constrictive spasm of the vagina, in painful retention of urine with spasm; *membranous dysmenorrhea.* Flow dark, clotted; intermittent. Better bending double and application of heat.

Enteralgia; *flatulent colic* forcing the patient to bend double; belching gives no relief. *Flatulent colic of children and newborns.* Diarrhoea, *watery* with vomiting and cramps in legs.

If there is continued vomiting accompanied by nausea. Asthma; spasmodic closure of wind pipe; constriction of chest and throat. In whooping cough for the continued "whoop" stage; if there is continued hiccough.

For St. Vitus' Dance; and in paralysis agitans; give *Mag-p.* as the needed tissue remedy.

Neuralgias of the face, stomach or bowels needs this remedy; also menstrual colic and ovarian neuralgia, painful membranous menstruation in alternation with doses of *Kali-m.* – conditions of spasm of the glottis, quinsy, the stabbing pains of goitre and for hypertrophy of the prostate gland. Should there be childbirth convulsions, *Mag-p.* is the required tissue remedy.

Doses of this tissue salt are indicated for phosphatic sediment in the urine; if there is itching over the whole body; for profuse perspiration and for brain exhaustion with insomnia, if this is accompanied with spasms.

Those who constitutionally appear to need this tissue salt as a remedy are the highly sensitive and nervous type of people, often thin and easily exhausted, and when in pain, sweat considerably.

In treating conditions of colic, convulsions and cramps, 6X potency is generally suitable and frequent doses in a little *hot water* is advised. In all other conditions needing this tissue salt, 3X potency is considered more suitable. In most cases, except those of established disability in paralysis agitans, St. Vitus' Dance, squinting, glandular diseases of goitre, prostate hypertrophy and the menstrual cycle, the condition needs to be treated as an acute one and frequent doses of this tissue salt are taken in *hot water,* since warmth gives additional efficacy. In dealing with these troubles with the 3-200X potency, however, large doses of ten to fifteen cellules will generally give better results.

Chronic conditions of disability, seen in continuing paralysis agitans, will generally need 30X potency, or even 200X or the 3-200X potency can be tried – one dose a day is suggested. These doses will probably need supporting trace elements in the prescription.

CHLORIDE OF SODA (NATRIUM MURIATICUM)

This mineral comprises the common salt of everyday use. It has a close affinity for water, dissolving in watery solution the otherwise insoluble phosphate of lime (*Calc-p.*) and regulating the amount of moisture in the body in its distribution throughout the tissues and intercellular spaces. It is a carrier of moisture to all cells– this is a requirement for cell growth and renewal.

Cells which do not contain this mineral are unable to attract water to themselves and *waterlogging in the intercellular spaces results (hydremia),* and is seen in conditions of *bloatedness,* with watery eyes or undue salivation. The person is languid, drowsy, lachrimose and chilly. Many of these individuals crave salt.

Common salt is one of the first needs of animals and human beings. All other mineral constituents of the body, as cell foods are dependent upon it for the process of their distribution and absorption. Salt is a constituent of every liquid and solid part of the body. It regulates the osmosis of water from arterial blood to serous sacs. A disturbance of function of these salt molecules is followed by a watery exudation within the sacs. Therapeutic application of *Nat-m.* enables the cells to reabsorb the exudation.

The particles of sodium chloride are split in the peptic glands and the sodium unites with carbonic acid (set free during the process of metabolism), entering the blood as sodium carbonate. The dissolved chlorine becomes hydrochloric acid, now a constituent of gastric juice required for dissolving food; dyspepsia is a result of deficient hydrochloric acid.

Malnutrition and emaciation, even while eating enormously. *Anemia,* leukemia, *chlorosis. Serous discharges. All mucous membranes affected,* causing sponginess, swelling with venous hydremia, bleeding and increased mucus secretion. Hence, catarrhs of all mucus membranes with secretion of *transparent, watery, coarse, frothy mucus. All diseases with watery, acrid, excoriating discharges* need this salt.

Dejection of spirits, *consolation aggravates. Depression* with tendency to dwell on depressing subjects. *Ready to shed tears. Hypochondriacal.* Melancholia at puberty. *Brain fag.*

Congestive headaches; dull, heavy with tears, drowsiness and unrefreshing sleep. Sick headache; hemicrania. *Hammering headache,*worse in the morning. *Itching eruption on margins of hair* at nape of neck. Dandruff. Falling off of hair with much dryness of scalp. Headache with eyestrain. *Sunstroke. Blepharitis,* with acrid lachrymation, *muscular asthenopia* of eyes. *Cracking in ears when chewing.*

Copious salivation with a salty taste. Blister-like pearls around the mouth. *Tongue, clean, shiny* or broad, puffy with a pasty coat. Mumps. Ulceration of the gums.

The imbalance is apparent in running colds and the watery type of influenza, hay fever. Loss of smell and taste. Asthma with edema.

Indicated in all fevers where there is watery vomit. *Intermittent fever after abuse of quinine* or living in damp regions.

This remedy is indicated in hydrocele, in epilepsy if the attack is accompanied by frothing and in pleurisy if this gives watery exudations.

Scrotal edema. Abundant leucorrhea of transparent, white, thick mucus or unnatural dryness of vagina. Uterine troubles relieved by lying on back, on pillow. In pregnancy, if the size of the breasts is excessive.

It is indicated in chronic facial eczema, nettle-rash (with *Kali-p.*), Itching violently; appears after physical exertion. Addison's disease for the skin conditions and exophthalmic goitre.

All affections with watery blisters or vesicles and thin, whitish scales. Greasy skin. Herpes. Warts an palms. Insect stings which give watery exudations. Cracked fingertips.

Waterbrash. Longing for salty food. *Violent thirst* for large quantities and *Ravenous hunger. Aversion to bread.* Neuralgia of the bowels. If chronic constipation is of a dry nature, with watery secretions, doses of this salt will quickly ease and cure the condition. Other conditions of constipation need the appropriate tissue salt and very probably a higher vitamin intake. *Torn, bleeding, smarting after stool, which is hard, difficult and crumbling* with stitches in rectum.

This tissue remedy is needed if individuals are habitually chilly with cold extremities from taking too much salt in the food. When there is numbness of the hands and feet, in sterility and in confinement when the mother's milk is watery and salty, doses of this salt is required.

Emaciated neck in children. *Backache*; better lying on something hard. If sciatica has not cleared with doses of *Kali-p.* and *Ferr-p.* there may be a constitutional need for this remedy, and it should be given in cases of hysteria, for stupor in illness, and for excessive heaviness of sleep or insomnia.[1] Dreams of robbers. All conditions where there is too much dryness or too much wateriness, showing an inbalance in the condition of natural moisture, indicate the need for this tissue remedy.

If the pulse is rapid and intermittent, and palpitation is present, or for the feeling of a constricted heart with fluttering, doses of this salt can be expected to bring the condition to normal.

With the exception of cold in the head, the sudden onset of hay fever, and that of collapse after exhaustion, generally respond to 6X potency. All other conditions needing this remedy are likely to require a 12X or 3-200X potency. For the acute condition of sunstroke give a dose of 12X or 3-200X potency every fifteen minutes.

Catarrhal fevers, mumps with salivation and dyspepsia, indicate a second stage inflammation, requiring a semi-acute treatment, and 12X potency is advised. For watery ulceration of the gums, for watery vomit, for frothy tongue and for dry constipation, these conditions of the digestive tract indicate the use of a high potency, and 3-200X is advised. Delirium, excessive heaviness of sleep and palpitations, also need a high potency, and much salivation with dribbling may require 200X.

All conditions requiring this tissue remedy are likely to respond well to the 3-200X potency.

PHOSPHATE OF SODA (NATRIUM PHOSPHORICUM)

The action of this salt in the body is to decompose lactic acid, which when not catalysed, irritates the tissues and causes much suffering in rheumatic subjects. In splitting the lactic acid into carbonic acid and water, the presence of this salt keeps the carbonic acid in the blood until it reaches the lungs, where it is given off in the exhaled breath. Hence, it is a remedy for conditions arising from excess of lactic acid.

The action of this salt in the tissue prevents the thickening of bile in the gall duct, assisting the assimilation of fats and preventing those conditions of jaundice and biliousness arising due to bile deficiency. Dyspeptic conditions traceable to fats.

This salt emulsifies and is the indicated remedy where fatty acids in the food disagree.

Nat-p. also keeps the normal uric acid soluble in blood. If this salt is out of balance, uric acid combines with soda that may be present and is deposited in the joints, producing the inflammation of rheumatism.

When there is acute rheumatism in the joints or there is gout, this tissue salt, is then indicated, and in some conditions of arthritis this is one of the remedies needed. (See also *Silicea*)

Conditions of nausea need this remedy; if underlying nervousness is present, *Kali-p.* should also be used. (These two salts are excellent remedies for travelling sickness.) Where the nausea is of a bilious character, the tissue remedy should be *Nat-s.* (See *Nat-s.* and the relationship between these two salts.)

Because of the presence of lactic acid condition, this tissue remedy is needed for sick headaches, especially if these are focused on top of the head, and where there is sour breath and sour vomits, with an acrid or coppery taste. This remedy is indicated where there is an offensive odour in front of the nose, and here the tissue salt *Mag-p.* is also needed. Nasal catarrh with thick, yellow, purulent discharge.

Ophthalmia, discharge of yellow, creamy matter. Lids glued together in the morning.

For heartburn, waterbrash and pain after food which goes through to the back; for flatulent risings which taste sour and for acidity which causes diarrhoea or frequent urination which is generally slight; for habitual constipation especially in children; if acid symptoms are present; for sterility if acidity symptoms are also present; for sour-smelling, creamy leucorrhea; for honey-colored secretions of eyes, and in eczema or pemphigus having these secretions; these conditions need suitable doses of this tissue salt.

Thin, moist coating on the back part of tongue and at the back part of the roof of the month.

Catarrh of thick yellow mucus – second stage of inflammation. If discharges are less thick but yellow and slimy,

Kali-s. is needed. Diabetic conditions indicate the need for this remedy, together with the use of *Nat-s.* Urine dark red with arthritis. Morning sickness with vomiting of sour fluids in pregnancy.

Where sleeplessness is accompanied by much itching and for the acid conditions of little children where there has been too much milk and sugar in the feeding, *Nat-p.* is the tissue remedy. Irritation of intestines by worms especially thread worms.

Goitre. Jaundice. Itching all over the body. Exudations and secretions yellow, honey-colored. Principal remedy in scrofulous glands, tuberculosis.

Where there are inflammation of a phlegmonous type (white leg), with swelling, owing to a breakdown in the activity of the white blood corpuscles, *Nat-p.* is the correct tissue remedy, but it needs to be taken promptly.

These conditions are mostly of an acute character and almost all can be expected to respond to a low potency of 3X. This will be suitable for vomiting from acidity, acute conditions of rheumatism, acidity of stomach, itching, ulceration of gums. If the conditions have persisted and there is continuing sleeplessness from acidity, continuing nausea, continuing sour sweats, a 6X potency is advised.

3-200X potency is applicable in all these conditions.

SULPHATE OF SODA (NATRIUM SULPHURICUM)

Sulphate of soda appears as a pharmaceutical product in the form of Glauber's salt. It is slightly irritant to the physical tissues and is used to stimulate natural secretions.

This salt in particle form is a constituent of the intercellular fluids of the body. Its function is to eliminate superfluous water from the system, including decomposition of products of lactic acid, which have been brought about by the action of *Nat-p*. (See *Nat-p*.)

Nat-m. has an affinity for water and carries moisture to the tissue cells; *Nat-s*. has similar attraction, but for that moisture which has become a product of retrograde processes,and which it draws to itself for elimination purposes. These two salts promote the balance in absorption and elimination of water necessary for the continuing life cycle of the cell tissues.

Nat-s. has a stimulating effect on the lining cells and the nerves of bile ducts, intestines and pancreas. It is consequently the remedy for biliousness, some types of constipation and flatulence, and becomes a nerves remedy in the relationship between the spleen, pancreas and solar plexus. It has a stimulating action on the "filtering" tubes of the urinary system in passing off unwanted water as urine. It increases the secretion of pancreatic fluid, and is of considerable importance as a remedy in conditions of diabetes. (See also *Nat-p*.)

Low fevers indicate a need for this tissue remedy. Bilious fevers.

Leucocytes remain too long in blood before disintegrating, resulting in leukemia. This tissue remedy withdraws their moisture and promotes the desired disintegration. The condition indicates an insufficiency of the particles of *Nat-s*.

Hydremia may be occasioned by an imbalance of this salt in the intercellular spaces; this condition is shown as edema of the tissues. *Nat-s*. corresponds to the hydrogenoid constitution. *Nat-s*. is indicated in complaints that are caused by *living in damp houses, basements and cellars*. Complaints are worse in wet weather from lying on the left side.

It's chief characteristic is a *dirty greenish-grey or greenish - brown coating of the root of the tongue*.

Suicidal tendency; *must exercise restraint.* Music aggravates symptoms. *Mental troubles arising from a fall or other injuries to the head.* Ill-effects of falls and injuries to the head.

Agglutination of the eyelids. Soapy taste in the mouth.

For sensation of burning in the nose, mouth and gums. Earache with noises in the ear.

Catarrhs with yellowish-green or green secretions.

Bilious vomiting with diarrhoea; bilious irritability with depression and despair. Sour rising heartburn. Dropsy from liver conditions; if the liver is tender from congestion, in jaundice, worse lying on left side. *Gall stones.* Flatulent colic. All discharges of watery pus, particularly from chronic conditions.

Soft warts and crops of warts around any part of the body; whitlows; these are also conditions which need doses of *Nat-s.*

This remedy should be used in bronchial asthma. *Humid asthma,* rattling of mucus. Dyspnea during damp weather.

Kidney disorders. *Chief remedy in diabetes. Gonorrhea and sycosis.* Retention and incontinence of urine.

Vomiting in pregnancy may need this remedy if *Nat-p.* and *Kali-p.* in alternation have not proved efficacious and where there is too much milk in lactation.

In rheumatic conditions suffered by hydremic patients. *spinal meningitis.* This tissue remedy will most probably be needed in phlegmasia alba-dolens with doses of *Nat-p.* (see *Nat-p.*) and in some conditions of constipation, particularly if this seems to be occasioned by a slimy catarrh.

If the tongue is coated greenish or dirty brown, needs *Nat-s.* The condition should be considered as acute and 3X potency should quickly clear it. The same potency is able to deal satisfactorily with the acute conditions of bilious colic, acute gout,

acute sciatica and bronchial asthma, if these individuals have
hydremic constitutions. Take frequent doses, half-hourly or every
fifteen to twenty minutes, until the condition is easier, and then
much less frequently until the trouble has cleared.

Conditions of nausea, vertigo, bilious or neuralgic sick
headaches, excessive sleepiness, noises in the ear, soft warts, soft
swellings, require doses of 6X potency, internally; difficult and
persisting cases will need higher potencies. Lotions of 3X potency
should be applied concurrently for soft warts and for the soft
swellings of erysipelas (with much soft bandaging).

Concussions from injuries may need a second remedy of *Nat-
s.* and a 6X potency is suggested (first remedy, give *Ferr-p.,* 3X
potency).

In all these conditions doses of the 3-200X potency are
applicable.

THE RELATIONSHIP BETWEEN CHLORIDE OF SODA, PHOSPHATE OF SODA AND SULPHATE OF SODA (NAT-M., NAT-P. AND NAT-S.)

Some of the indications for *Nat-m.* as a remedy will also
appear to require *Nat-s.* These salts are closely associated in their
actions within the body. *Nat-m.* has the power of attracting
moisture to the cells and the intercellular spaces and of regulating
the amount there; *Nat-s.* withdraws, retrograde and superfluous
moisture. The symptoms of "wateriness" however are heavier and
thicker in texture or of a slimy nature (being retrograde), when
the requirement is for *Nat-s.*

When nausea presents itself as the chief symptom of illness,
we have to decide whether the needed mineral nutrient is *Nat-p.*
or *Nat-s.* Because of its emulsifying action, *Nat-p.* is the remedy
when fatty foods disagree or there is excess of lactic acid.

Some conditions of nausea and sickness are precipitated by purely nervous factors; in these cases *Kali-p.* needs to be taken as well as doses of *Nat-p.*

Nat-s. is given where biliousness is caused by the decomposition of lactic acid not having been eliminated from the system. *Nat-s.* is not, strictly speaking, a cell salt, but a constituent of the intercellular fluids. It attracts superfluous water in the system to itself and is the factor which causes elimination of the fluid. The superfluous water is a decomposition product. The action of *Nat-s.* in the intercellular fluids follows that of *Nat-p.* in the tissue cells.

SILICIC ACID (SILICEA)

Silicic acid is a constituent of all the connective tissue cells of the body, hair, nails and skin. This connective tissue covers the brain, spinal cord and nerve fibres. When there is an imbalance of *Silicea* in these tissues, swelling and inflammation result, with pain. The effect of these disturbances, however, may be absorbed through the lymphatics or suppuration may ensure before it is resolved. Suitable doses of *Silicea* will promote the essential absorption.

A deficiency of *Silicea* in the connective tissues causes a lack of an essential nutrient of the brain and nerves, resulting in poor memory, slow and difficult thoughts, absent-mindedness. *Silicea* is contained in the epidermis of wheat and other cereals. Eating whole grain products should provide the normal need for this element.

This tissue salt is able to dissolve urate of soda (the "poisons") deposited in so many arthritic joints. The capacity for absorption is determined by the condition of lymphatics. Most of these vessels have valves to assist the return of lymph and waste products from the tissues to the veins, and their function of good drainage and absorption reflects in the health of these tissues.

If uric acid is present in the urine, this tissue salt should be taken in small doses until the trouble disappears.

A remedy for ailments attended with *pus formation;* in all *fistulous burrowings.* It *promotes suppuration.* In third stage inflammation. In neglected cases of injury if suppuration threatens. Fungi. Easily bleeding abscesses. Tendency for enlarged suppurating glands, especially cervical gland. Skin heals with difficulty. Ulceration and necrosis of bones as in jaws, mastoid, nasal bone, etc.

Symptoms are always worse at night and during full moon. *Better by heat, warm room* and in summer. Worse, cold air and suppressed foot sweat.

Indications for *Silicea* are dry feet with an offensive odour, showing a lack of natural perspiration; night-sweats, particularly of the head and any condition of over-perspiration of feet, arm-pits, with much odour. Doses of *Silicea* should restore the condition to one of normal perspiration without noticeable odour.

All conditions of poor nourishment and weakness, with general irritability caused by defective assimilation of food – indicate a need for this nutrient remedy. General debility indicates a need for this tissue salt, in combination with *Calc-p.*

Silicea promotes suppuration; boils, carbuncles indicate a need for this tissue salt. It is generally *contraindicated* in appendicitis and in torpor of nerves.

Those who get tired easily, physically, who are sensitive to much internal chilliness, who have little body heat, those whose menses is accompanied with icy coldness and probably constipation, who easily get headaches from study, nervous exhaustion or digestive conditions, need doses of this tissue nutrient.

Oversensitive to noise. Headache from nape of neck to vertex, more on right side. Crusta lactea with offensive oozing. Epilepsy at night; aura begins in the solar plexus. Exhaustion with erethism.

If the hair falls out, for conditions of cataract and styes, because of the connective tissues involved, and for some conditions of deafness, this tissue nutrient is the correct remedy.

Where there is ulceration of the nasal bones with discharge, ulceration of the mouth and tongue. Thickening of mucous membranes generally with blockage. Otorrhea. Sneezing, nasal catarrh. Ozena with fetid, offensive discharge.

This tissue salt has been called the surgeon of biochemistry. It clears foul discharges, fetid diarrhoea and excretions. It is used for encysted tumors, hard gatherings with pain, ankylosis. Occupational diseases of stone-workers and coal-miners where the dust gets into the bronchi and lungs, need this "surgical" tissue remedy. All irritating, difficult coughs, where there is much trouble in clearing the expectoration, indicate the need for this remedy.

Suppurative stage of pneumonia. Empyema. Suppurative, rattling, loose, copious expectoration of thick, yellow-green pus with hectic fever, profuse night sweats and great debility.

Hectic fever during long suppurative processes. *Chilliness* all day, want of animal heat. *Heat* in afternoon and all night with burning in feet. *Sweat at night* with prostration.

Brittle nails, ribbed, ingrowing nails need this salt. Chilblains. *Lepra*. Eczemas.

Large abdomen in children. *Constipation; stools recede after having been partially expelled. Fissure in anus* and *anal fistula.*

Suppuration of kidneys; chronic catarrh of bladder; urine loaded with pus and mucus. Chronic gonorrhea.

Menses associated with icy coldness of the body, constipation and fetid footsweat. Leucorrhea acrid, profuse, itching.

Mastitis. Scirrhus. Nipples crack and ulcerate easily. Fistulous ulcers of mammae, hard lumps of mammae with threatening suppuration.

Obstinate neuralgia, soreness or tenderness of feet giving lameness[1], *irritation of spine,* bruised or diseased bones; chronic synovitis, chronic conditions of weak ankles. Spinal curvature; Pott's disease. *Whitlow, felon.* Rheumatic and arthritic concretions. Caries of bones with fistulous opening. Tonic spasm of hand when writing; and feet and toes during a long walk.

Chronic sleeplessness from congestion of blood; these persisting conditions are likely to require *Sil.*

Spasm of sphincter ani with partial expulsion and receding of stools; stricture of the lachrymal ducts need suitable doses of *Silicea.*

All elderly people have a general need for *Silicea.*

The more deep-rooted conditions of ulcerations, diseased bone, inflammation of the breasts, chronic rheumatism and arthritis, tumors, need doses of *Silicea* in the comparatively high potency of 12X. All other conditions needing this tissue remedy can be expected to clear with the 6X potency. 3-200X potency is applicable in all cases; two or three doses a day are generally suitable. Any specially difficult condition might well require experienced attendance.

REFERENCE :

1.   Less salt food is usually desirable.

CHAPTER 4

The Importance of Food Balance in Daily Meals: Table of some Comparative Food Values

The importance of a balanced meal cannot be undermined. This not only refers to the protein, carbohydrate and fat content, but also to the equally essential mineral and vitamin factors as well.

Individual requirements regarding the quantity of food eaten varies widely, according to age, physical conditions, occupational needs, personal tastes and the whole attitude towards the question of feeding oneself. This last is generally a matter of habit or of emotions. Many people are conservative in food and tend to follow the pattern passed on by their parents. Emotional reactions, often unconscious, govern the choice of food, on how much is sufficient, and on its association and attraction values when and how it comes on the table.

When a meal is not properly balanced in its content, some part of its nutritive value is lost. Too much of certain foods may be taken, and too little of certain essential foods to ensure the proper assimilation of the whole. Thus, starch in order to be properly digested needs its complement of vitamin B_1, otherwise the end product, glucose, will be incompletely oxidized, in which case toxins accumulate in the blood and poison the nerves. The choice of whole-grain foods in a meal provides the carbohydrate content and the vitamin B_1, since this vitamin is present in the outer skins of the grain. There is a similar reason for cooking potatoes with their skins thereby retaining most of that vegetable's mineral salts. The natural salts and vitamin factors contained in vegetables and fruits are *essential* for the health of the human body.

The body requires protein to supply its nitrogen needs. The nitrogen obtained from protein intake has to equal the loss of nitrogen through the process of wear and tear of body's tissues. The protein intake has to also supply essential constituents for the body's metabolic changes and for building new tissue. Proteins contain approximately sixteen percent nitrogen. Some contain much less, but a mixture of protein foods will invariably supply the average need for nitrogen.

The process of metabolism requires protein, but this activity cannot proceed correctly without the presence of carbohydrates. When carbohydrates are not taken at the same meal, the protein break-down in the liver is burnt to sugars and the body's protein needs for tissue repair and tissue building are not met. If protein is consumed in excess, the balance is wasted in liver sugar and the body may suffer a protein deficiency later. Though predominantly of one structure or another, most foods contain some amounts of protein, carbohydrate, fat, some minerals and vitamins, all in close association.

Foods assist one another in the process of metabolism and a mixed diet best keeps the metabolism in balance. Too much protein and particularly too much animal protein, quickens the rate of metabolism. This is likely to advance the ageing process. Too little protein and rather too much carbohydrate and fat is likely to cause obesity from too little combustion of this material and its consequent deposit in the tissues.

Scientific research and experiments appear to show that 1 gram of protein per kilogram of body weight is needed daily. This means that 2½ oz. of actual protein is needed daily by a man weighing 11 stones (st.) and 2 oz. of actual protein is needed daily by a woman of 8 st. 12 lb. But the British Medical Association and the Conference of the Food and Agricultural Organization in 1944 recommended that these figures should be raised a little to probably 3½ oz. for a man weighing 11 st. and to 3 oz. for a woman of 8 st. 12 lb. These are *actual protein figures* and *not* the weight of foods containing protein.

The quality of protein is another important factor. Dairy foods, classed as animal protein are more wholely broken down and assimilated by the human tissues than pure vegetable proteins. From the health point of view, it is well to observe that the end products of *flesh* proteins occasion putrefaction in the human bowel, and those from starch and vegetable foods give rise to fermentation, providing very obvious reasons for daily evacuations, which should be natural and adequate.

Experiments have shown that the greatest biological value is obtained if half the protein food eaten is from vegetable and half from animal sources; that the amount of actual flesh foods eaten should be limited; and in all cases it should be offset with fresh vegetables and fruit to give adequate mineral and vitamin content.

Carbohydrates and fats consist of carbon, hydrogen and oxygen, and are energy foods. They are needed to burn (break down) the proteins to obtain nitrogen release and convert it to the body's needs and are a necessary link in the process of metabolism. Carbohydrates, too, are essential in the structure of body tissues. If carbohydrates and fats are eaten in excess of the body's requirement, they are stored in the tissues. Fats are not properly converted into energy unless sufficient carbohydrates are also eaten, carbohydrates give bulk to a diet; fats give a greater feeling of satiaty.

Nutritionists have believed that a high fat intake has some relationship with the incidence of coronary and vascular diseases and the investigations carried out by the American, Dr. Ancel Keys, appear to show conclusively that this is so.

It is considered that a high cholesterol level in blood is the causative factor in the degeneration of arteries and an excessive fat deposition in the liver. Cholesterol is a sterol found in combination with fatty acids. Foods which have a good cholesterol content are eggs, liver, kidney and fats (including cream). It is generally inadvisable to eat much of these foods unless there is exceptionally good oxidation, particularly so of the fats.

Carbohydrates eaten at the same meal aid oxidation of fats and other factors of metabolism assist in this process; exercise is a factor in the conversion of fat compounds and the accompanying carbohydrates into energy, but not necessarily the cholesterol factor in the fats.

Cholesterol is a constituent of blood, of the covering of nerve fibres, of the sebum of skin glands, of the bile, and is found in all the cells and body fluids. In the blood and in the skin glands it has protective value. In some circumstances it crystallizes and forms gall-stones from too great a concentration in the gall-bladder.

Dr. Keys also found that "a low fat intake and low values for cholesterol in the blood go together". Fat stimulates the liver to make cholesterol. It was also found that "fats from meat and dairy products are the highest promoters of sebum cholesterol; fish oils and some vegetable oils promote the cholesterol level". Maize oil apparently does not.

Sunshine and the use of ultraviolet lamps, have the effect of changing the cholesterol into vitamin D within the body. Vitamin D is an essential factor in the absorption of the body's calcium, and promotes the cycle of metabolism. (See also vitamin D values and sources of this vitamin in food) This process, however, should not be allowed to become exhaustive, since the body has both its cholesterol as well as its vitamin D requirements. Sunshine or the use of an ultraviolent lamp can lower cholesterol content in the body. It is also relatively easy to lower the fat intake (and the cholesterol level) by omitting cream from the diet and controlling the butter and animal fat intake.

The following food balance is suggested:

Protein foods	:	4-6 oz. daily, depending on the foods chosen and individual needs.
Carbohydrate foods	:	Probably 8 oz. or more, daily. This is difficult to determine; more will be needed if a high protein intake is usual, in order to metabolize the protein successfully.
Fats	:	8 oz. butter (or other fat and oil) per week.
Fruits and vegetables	:	8 oz. or more, daily; and an orange and a tomato are recommended each day.
Additional	:	1 pint of milk daily is generally considered advisable, taken in tea, coffee or used in combination with other food or taken, itself, as a drink.

Protein foods from animal sources include fresh and dried milk, various cheese, eggs, fish, fowl and meat. Vegetable proteins include various nuts, soya flour, whole-grain cereals and pulse foods.

Carbohydrate foods which, in addition to their starch or sugar content, largely retain the vitamins and mineral elements natural to their organism, are the wholemeal or high-extract flours for bread, biscuits and cakes; oats; unpolished rice; dry fruits; honey; black treacle and the Barbados sugar or "pieces" sugar; potatoes when cooked in their skins (except when they have become "old" at the end of their season and have lost their vitamin C content); and pulses.

Pulse foods consist of a high concentration of carbohydrate and a lesser concentration of protein; this occurs also in fresh peas, since these are all seeds.

Most fruits and vegetables are predominantly mineral and vitamin foods, except those that more particularly have value for their starch and protein content, namely peas, beans, potatoes and root vegetables.

Full-cream milk, cheese and nuts, contain high percentages of fat, as well as protein content. A liberal use of these foods in the diet obviates the need for a higher butter allowance than that shown at 8 oz. a week.

All foods are complex in structure and if not unduly processed retain various proportions of carbohydrates, protein, minerals and vitamins, natural to their structure. Black treacle, for instance, consists of 28.5 percent water, 67.2 percent sugar, 0.19 percent nitrogen, 1.2 percent protein and high contents of the minerals—sodium, potassium, calcium, magnesium, iron, copper, phosphorus, sulphur and chlorine. The amount used with food is very small, but it is taken primarily for its mineral and sugar content, the mineral factor being of value for the blood and the bowels.

In considering any tables of values for the various foods, the actual amount eaten has to be remembered and how often a particular food is acceptable in the daily meals. Nuts give a higher protein value than peas, beans and pulses and with considerably less carbohydrate proportion. However, generally a less amount of nuts is eaten (and not all the protein is well digested).

The value of a meal, as well as the pleasures of the palate, depend on how the different foods are mixed and the amounts taken. Potatoes and nuts served at the same meal to supply the protein and carbohydrate food provide only second-class protein and low vitamin content; also, the mineral content would be somewhat inadequate since we have to remember the calcium in the nuts is only partly assimilable; and such a dish would give little flavor for the palate. The phytates in the nuts would be offset, if watercress or a green vegetable were included, and this would raise the mineral and vitamin content to a more satisfactory level.

Simple though it may be, a poached egg on buttered brown toast, with watercress or bread and butter and a firm cheese and some well-chosen fruit give a better-balanced meal in every respect. The egg, the cheese, provide the animal or first-class protein, and the bread gives vegetable protein and the necessary balance of carbohydrates. The essential mineral and vitamin content, in addition to that supplied by the egg, the cheese, bread and butter, is augmented by the watercress or the fruit, which might well be an orange or a tomato.

The energy of the universe is convertible. Plants use light from the sun to make proteins, starches and sugars, thus converting energy into their tissues. Man and animals eat these plants and in the process of digestion the energy of the plants are liberated and converted by the process of metabolism into the type of energy we need.

Breathing needs energy; the flow of blood round the body to all the tissues needs energy in the ceaseless action of the heart muscle. It takes energy to slough off old skin and make new tissues. All external work, too, needs energy, talking, household tasks, mental and manual work. The activities of standing and sleeping take energy. Digested products of food unite with oxygen which has been released in the breakdown of that food as also with that taken in the breath, and result in the release of heat and production of new tissue. This heat supplies energy for work and is a part of the process of metabolism. The actual work of digestion uses energy. The body cannot utilize all the food it eats and some is excreted as waste – that too, requires energy

TABLE OF COMPARATIVE FOOD VALUES

		Protein %	Fat %	Available Carbohydrate %	Water %
*Butter		0.4	85.1	Trace	13.9
Cheese	Cheddar	24.9	34.5	Trace	37.0
	Dutch	28.1	16.8	Trace	46.3
	Gorgonzola	24.8	31.1	Trace	41.0
	St. Ivel	23.1	30.5	Trace	45.7
	Stilton	25.1	40.0	Trace	28.2
	Gruyère	36.8	33.4	Trace	21.9
	Cream cheese	3.2	42.0	2.4	53.0
Eggs	Boiled	11.9	12.3	Nil	73.4

	Poached	12.4	11.7	Nil	74.7
Milk	Dried	26.4	29.7	38.8	1.3
	Fresh Milk	3.3	3.7	4.8	87.0
Nuts	Almonds	20.5	53.5	4.3	4.7
(all	Barcelonas	12.9	64.0	5.2	5.7
shelled)	Brazils	13.8	61.5	4.1	8.5
	†Cashews	21.5	52.5	5(approx.)	7.2
	Chestnuts	2.3	2.7	36.6	51.7
	Peanuts	28.1	49.0	8.6	4.5
	Walnuts	12.5	51.5	5.0	23.5
Beans	Broad, boiled	4.1	Trace	7.1	83.7
	Butter, boiled	7.1	Trace	17.1	70.5
	French, boiled	0.8	Trace	1.1	95.5
	Haricot, boiled	6.6	Trace	16.6	69.6
	Runner, boiled	0.8	Trace	0.9	93.6
Peas	Fresh, boiled	5.0	Trace	7.7	80.0
	Dried, boiled	6.9	Trace	19.1	70.3
	Split, dried, boiled	8.3	Trace	21.9	67.3
Soya	flour, full fat	40.3	23.5	26.6‡	7.0
	flour, grits	49.6	7.2	34.4‡	7.0
Flour	brown, mixed grist	11.6	1.9	74.2	15.0
	Bread made from it	8.3	1.4	53.3	39.0

*   Average figures taken from English, Empire and Forign samples.

†   After removed of brown pericarp.

‡   And dextrin.

		Protein %	Fat %	Available Carbohydrate %	Water %
Flour	mixed grist (80%)	11.2	1.4	77.6	15.0
	Bread made from it mixed grist, white	8.3	1.0	57.5	37.0
	(70%)	10.8	1.1	78.9	15.0
	Bread made from it	8.1	0.8	59.3	36.0
Oatmeal	raw	12.1	8.7	72.8	8.9
Bacon	back rashers, fried	24.6	53.4		12.7
	gammon, fried	31.3	33.9		24.9
Beef	steak, raw	19.3	10.5		68.3
	steak, grilled	25.2	21.6		50.5
	topside, roast, lean and fat	24.2	23.8		50.0
Chicken	boiled, flesh	26.2	10.3		61.0
Mutton	chop, lean, grilled	26.5	17.5		53.7
	leg, roast	25.0	20.4		52.4
Kidney	ox, rast	17.0	5.3		75.5
	sheep, raw	16.8	3.1		77.4
Liver	raw, mixed samples	16.5	8.1		73.3
Cod	middle cut, steamed	18.0	0.9		79.2
Cod	grilled, with added butter	27.0	5.3		64.6
Plaice	raw fillets	15.3	1.8		80.8
	steamed, body of fish	18.1	1.9		78.0

Mineral ash, etc., additional.

Statistics from *Chemical Composition of Foods* by McCance and Widdowson, published by H.M.S.O. and from *Biochemical Journal*, **30**, 1936, for cashew nuts.

CHAPTER 5

The Body's Need of Mineral Elements: Foods Which Supply These Elements

Mineral elements present in the human body, in addition to carbon, hydrogen and oxygen, consist of major amounts of calcium, phosphorus, potassium, sulphur, chlorine, sodium and magnesium, and much smaller amounts of iron, manganese, iodine. Many others are essential constituents, but only in "trace" amounts and of these the more usually recognized are cobalt, silicon, aluminium, arsenic, boron, copper, fluorine, nickel and zinc.

Though the amounts present vary considerably from approximately 2 lb. of calcium to only 2.8 gram of iron and 0.028 gram of iodine[1], this is no measurement of their value in the human body, for without its calcium there would be no structure, and without its iron there would be no blood.

It is probable that all the constituents of the atmosphere, the seas and the soil, enter in infinitesimal amounts into living physical tissue, through the food and the breath, and are essential for full function. All these are not traceable in discernible amounts in human tissue, but it has been found that many diseases have been cured when given an extremely high potency, i.e. a very fine trituration of a "trace" element to act as a synergist, a co-ordinating element, to another factor in the prescription.

This is seen to be true when a minute amount of the trace element arsenic is added to a prescription of *Kali-p*. Without the arsenic, the *Kali-p*. remains inert in those individuals whose phosphorus metabolism requires this synergist. Sufferers with chronic asthma may require just this metabolism correction.

The minerals required most by the body are calcium and phosphorus, iron and iodine. If the supplies of these are adequate it may be considered that the body's mineral requirement are *probably* being met. Foods which contain calcium, phosphorus and iron cover a relatively wide range, and those other essential mineral constituents of the physical tissues are generally found in association with them. The iodine requirement may well need separate consideration.

In nature, these minerals vitamins and "trace" elements are absorbed into the tissues of the plants, animals and fish. A variety of food in the daily meals is most likely to provide all the factors which the physical tissues need for healthy metabolism. If the meals are deficient in various food factors some part of the metabolic process, will suffer, with a sub-standard of nutrition in the cell life, the digestive juices or the intercellular fluids.

If inflammation and disease invade the physical tissues, disturbing the mineral particles, these minerals and the required "trace" elements, when correctly prepared and prescribed as tissue remedies, effect a particular balance, which if not already irrevocable – and this is unusual if taken in time – can be expected to restore health. Suitable nutrition becomes a co-operative factor.

CALCIUM AND PHOSPHORUS

The mineral element most extensively found in the human body is calcium. Every adult needs an approximately 0.8 grams of calcium daily. Additional calcium is needed by women during pregnancy, lactation – since some of their own calcium is given with the milk, and by growing children. These additional needs have been estimated to bring these requirements to a level of 1.4 grams daily.

The body excretes about 0.5 grams of calcium daily; and the 0.3 grams of the estimated normal daily requirement for adults has to provide the necessary margin to meet all the body's demands.

The body distributes its intake of calcium not only to the bones and teeth, which are formed of calcium and phosphorus in the growing stages and are constantly having their calcium replaced, but also to the blood for the process of normal clotting, the digestive juice and to the organic tissues including the heart muscle (calcium is a factor in ensuring muscular contraction).

Calcium combines with albumen to form new blood cells, bone tissue and teeth, though this does not necessarily appear in the adult as a new set of teeth. Renewed gastric juice is also formed from the combination of calcium with albumen.

Foods having a high content of calcium are easily remembered, being skimmed milk powders, cheese, eggs, fish in which bones are edible and watercress. One pint of milk gives 0.68 grams one egg will give approximately 0.45 grams; and cheese should give 0.23 grams per oz. Analysed figures for foods with the highest content of calcium are:

	mg. per oz.
Skimmed milk powder	348
Fresh milk	34
Cheese	230
Eggs	17 (per oz.)
Whitebait	240
Tinned sardines	113
Watercress	63
National and white breads	30
Herrings	28
Cabbage	18
Turnips	17
Cauliflower	14
Cod	7
Wholemeal bread (100% extraction)	6

Where there is an imbalance in calcium distribution or a definite deficiency in the calcium intake, either slight or serious, deficiency diseases result.

If too much sugar is taken, the blood is robbed of its calcium. This is because the body attempts to neutralize the effects of excess sugar by drawing on the calcium already present in the blood, teeth, joints, etc. Excess sugar will also rob the body tissues of oxygen, which it demands for its combustion in the tissues. However, oxygen is required for all the body's moderate demands, including that of carrying minerals and vitamins to all its tissues.

Too much fat in the diet will prevent full absorption of calcium. The presence of oxalic acid and phytic acid in certain foods also prevents full calcium absorption. Oxalic acid is notably found in spinach and in rhubarb, and if these two products are served with calcium foods – cheese, eggs, milk custards – the oxalic acid combines with the calcium and forms an insoluble salt, calcium oxalate. It is probable, however, that if a sufficiently liberal amount of cheese or milk custard is taken with these foods, the additional calcium intake will more than compensate for the insoluble calcium oxalate.

The same neutralization should be observed in serving wholemeal bread with cheese, because of the phytates in the bread and whole-grain cereals, e.g., oatmeal with milk. Some of the phytic acid present with the calcium content in pulse vegetables and whole-grain cereals, however, is destroyed in the various cooking processes these foods may be subjected to.

Effective assimilation of calcium foods may require a prescription of Nat-m. especially if there is some gastric trouble, or in convalescence after illness.

The elderly frequently suffer from insufficient calcium and this sometimes occasions rheumatic-like pains in their muscles and joints. If bones break easily in persons of all ages and if fractures are slow to heal, this is generally an indication for the need of additional calcium.

The absorption of adequate amount of calcium by the human body and its distribution in the blood and tissues depends upon its intake of phosphorus, the presence of vitamin D, and normal activity of the parathyroid glands. These glands act as a balancing mechanism in controlling the calcium level in blood. This level should remain constant, the bones acting as a "bank" from which calcium for the blood can be withdrawn, or where excess calcium can be temporarily deposited.

Phosphorus is found in close association with calcium and the question of adequate supplies does not arise irrespective of the calcium intake. Not only is phosphorus concerned closely with calcium in the formation of bones and teeth and in their renewal processes, but it assists the processes of metabolism by which energy is released from food. Phosphorus also stabilizes the composition of body's fluids.

There is a good content of phosphorus in almost all foods. Those which give the highest figures are:

	mg. per oz.
Cheese	155
Oatmeal	108
Eggs	62
National bread	28
Milk	28
Cabbage	18

Vitamin D assists in correcting the ratio of calcium to phosphorus supply taken from food. The presence of vitamin D in the body is essential for the successful absorption of calcium. A small intake of calcium in the daily meals, having the vitamin D factor also present a greater value to the body than a large amount of calcium without its co-operating factor, vitamin D. Vitamin D renders the small amount of calcium wholly assimilable; a large amount of calcium if taken with insufficient vitamin D will probably causes calcium dificiency. Where there is insufficient vitamin D, there are sure to be signs of calcium deficiency.

Vitamin D also promotes the health of the skin; sunlight and ultraviolet irradiation are used therapeutically for certain skin diseases. Vitamin D is manufactured within the body by the action of sunlight on the skin, by the use of ultraviolet lamps – exposure needs careful supervision – and by the inclusion of foods which contain this vitamin in the daily meals. This vitamin is not found in many foods, it is, however, resistant to cooking and no loss need to be expected. Foods which contain this vitamin are:

	International Units per oz.
Tunny fish oil ⎫	Used as dietary supplements and
Halibut liver oil ⎬	for therapeutric purposes 5,400,
Cold liver oil ⎭	5,670, and above, per oz.
Sardines	280
Herrings	250
Tinned salmon	170
Margarine (added synthetically)	90
Eggs	17
Butter	17
Cheese	4
Milk (fresh)	0.1–0.7 (seasonal variation)

Some milk powders have added vitamin content and details are given on their labels.

The adult requirement for vitamin D has not been fixed and it would be extremely difficult to make a general assessment. If, however, an adult is suffering from nutritional debility or has a deficiency disease because of some imbalance in assimilation (poor assimilation of calcium is probably a contributing factor in some cases of rheumatism), additional vitamin D is generally indicated.

The daily requirement for this vitamin by growing children has been estimated as 500 International Units. It is considered that the elderly are able to convert calcium from any such deposits within their tissues upto a late age. Obviously to do this, adequate amounts of vitamin D are required and it would appear unwise to estimate the required intake as very much lower than 500 I.U. for any age. The vitamin is concerned also in preventing caries of the teeth, a point which can be of increasing interest to all ages.

The body is able to store this vitamin to draw upon as its needs require.

Calcium occurs in the body in two forms, calcium carbonate and calcium phosphate. The latter is a compound of calcium and phosphorus. The body's requirement for calcium and phosphorus is closely related.

Calcium carbonate is considered a suitable form of calcium for adding to wheat flours, other than the 100 percent extraction. The argument is that the added calcium offsets the harmful effects of the phytates present in the higher extraction flours and needs to be added to the low extraction (white) flours on account of their de-mineralization in the milling process.

The 100 percent extraction wheat flour free of the added calcium carbonate was agreed in response to a minority's plea that their bread should be neither added to nor subjected to de-mineralization processes.

It seems a pity, however, that calcium phosphate and silica in a potency of possibly 3X cannot be introduced in preference to calcium carbonate. This procedure is likely to retard ageing, since in the tissues of old people the silica content diminishes and carbonates form in their place – this being, in fact, a process of ageing.

IRON

The iron requirement of the body has been given as 0.004 percent of the body's weight. The average amount found in the body of a man weighing 11 st. os 0.09 oz. or 2.8 grams. Authoritative figures give the needs of adult men and women for iron as 12 milligrams a day, with adolescents, nursing mothers and those in pregnancy needing 15 milligrams.

The body is able to store very little of its iron and foods containing this requirement should be included in the daily meals. In general, these foods are whole-grain flours, whole-grain cereals, egg-yolk, beef liver, green vegetables and some fruits.

Some of the iron in food is not assimilable, but inorganic iron is absorbed and in this form it occurs in certain fruits, green vegetables, liver, kidney, white fish and eggs. Insufficient hydrochloric acid in the digestive juices may prevent iron absorption from even the assimilable iron foods.

Iron is apparently best absorbed by the physical tissues in the form of ferrous iron, and it is the presence of ascorbic acid – vitamin C – in the intestine which facilitates its absorption by changing one form of iron into another, the ferric ions into ferrous ions.

The limited storage of iron in the body, and its utilization as required by the tissues depend upon the substance apoferritin in the intestinal mucous membrane. The full capacity of this protein for taking up iron is easily reached, and in consequence the body's supplies of assimilable iron need daily replenishment through well-chosen foods. It will be appreciated also that intestinal health is a contributing feature of iron absorption.

The following table gives a list of foods with a good iron content and, as well, the percentage rate of this which is assimilable iron. Those foods with the highest content are marked with an asterisk for easier reference. The other foods shown in this list, when used during the full complement of the day's meals, provide a useful contribution to that day's assimilable iron content. For purposes of interest and comparison, some figures for flesh foods are also included. These contain good sources of organic iron, but, as will be seen, little of this is actually assimilable by the body.

These figures may show small variations for the various foodstuffs, but the authors of the analysis advise us that they can be accepted with confidence (*Biochemic journal, 30*). Figures for raw and cooked food are given in some cases to show small variations in the figure content when subjected to cooking and other processes.

Note. – Sherman's figures give the daily standard allowance as 1.32 grams phosphorus, 0.68 grams calcium, 0.012 grams iron: *Chemistry of Food and Nutrition,* by H. C. Sherman.

TABLE OF FOODS SHOWING THE TOTAL IRON IN MG. PER 100 G. OF THE FOOD: ALSO THE PERCENTAGE OF THE TOTAL IRON WHICH IS ASSIMILABLE

	Total iron in mg. per 100 g.	Assimilable iron % of total iron
Vegetables:		
Artichoke, globe, cooked	0.55	100
Beans, broad, raw	*1.08	93
butter, cooked	*1.82	71
French, raw	0.57	87
haricot, cooked	*2.72	84
scarlet runner, cooked	*0.74	74
tinned, baked	*2.05	98
Beetroot, cooked	0.50	94
Brussels sprouts, raw	0.67	75
Cabbage, cooked	0.87	70
Carragheen moss	*8.88	97

	Total iron in mg. per 100 g.	*Assimilable iron % of total iron*
Vegetables:		
Carrot, raw	*0.56	100
cooked	0.41	98
Cauliflower, cooked	0.52	100
Celeriac, cooked	*0.87	98
Celery, raw	0.14	100
Chicory, raw	0.57	66
Cucumber, raw	0.25	100
Endive, raw	*2.77	72
Fennel, raw, fresh	*4.20	50
raw, dry	*9.06	45
Leek, raw	*0.77	91
Lentil, raw	*7.63	60
Lettuce, raw	0.80	63
Mushroom, raw	0.65	100
Mustard and cress, raw	*5.70	45
Parsley, raw	*10.00	50
Peas, cooked	*1.55	77
split, cooked	*1.84	71
tinned	*2.10	100
Radish, raw	*1.68	65
Salsify, raw	*1.33	98
Sea kale	0.66	91
Spinach, cooked	*4.15	67
Watercress, raw	*2.08	66

	Total iron in mg. per 100 g.	Assimilable iron % of total iron
Fruits:		
Apricot, dry, raw	*4.08	98
fresh, raw	0.37	95
Avocado pear, raw	0.53	100
Banana, raw	0.47	100
Blacberry, raw	0.95	41
Cherry, raw	0.48	100
Currant, black, raw	*0.95	100
red, raw	0.66	85
Custard apple, raw	0.52	100
Damson, raw	0.63	70
Date, dry	*1.71	82
Fig, dry, raw	*4.17	96
Grape, as raisins	*3.80	97
as sultana	*3.60	65
Greengage, raw	0.46	84
Loganberry, raw	*1.00	76
Medlar, raw	0.77	65
Mulberry, raw	1.57	50
Nectarine, raw	0.46	87
Passion fruit, raw	*1.12	100
Peach, dry, raw	*7.60	92
fresh, raw	0.39	100
Plum, as prunes, raw	*3.20	72

	Total iron in mg. per 100 g.	Assimilable iron % of total iron
Raspberry, raw	*1.11	82
Strawberry	0.71	52
Tomato, raw	0.37	53
Nuts:		
Almond	*4.54	99
Barcelona	*3.44	91
Brazil	*2.70	61
Cob	*1.44	94
Chestnut	0.87	60
Peatnut	*1.19	100
Walnut	*1.83	41
Coconut	*1.98	86
Cereals:		
Biscuit, digestive	*1.57	91
Ryvita	*3.20	100
Bread, wholemeal	*3.43	83
"Hovis"	*2.48	95
Oatmeal	*4.15	96
Miscellaneous:		
Cocoa	*14.20	93
Chocolate, plain	*1.67	84
milk	*3.28	89
Treacle, golden syrup	*1.68	95

	Total iron in mg. per 100 g.	Assimilable iron % of total iron
black	*9.17	100
Egg, raw	*2.50	100

Flesh foods:

	Total iron in mg. per 100 g.	Assimilable iron % of total iron
Fish, Cod, raw	0.34	100
Haddock, steamed	*0.75	100
Halibut, raw	0.44	100
Herring, fried	*1.02	74
Mackerel, fried	*1.17	64
Plaice, steamed	0.68	97
Salmon, tinned	*0.89	94
Sardines, tinned	*3.44	65
Skate, raw	0.33	100
Sole, steamed	0.45	100
Winkles, boiled	*10.4	58
Heart, baked	*5.83	63
Kadney, ox, stewed	*4.92	66
pig, fried	*9.50	58
Liver, calf's, raw	*13.30	100
lamb's, fried	*2.76	100
ox, raw	·*6.70	78
pig's, raw	*20.00	80
Sweetbreads, raw	*1.47	71

Flesh foods having good organic iron content, but low percentages of assimilable iron:	Total iron in mg. per 100 g.	Assimilable iron % of total iron
Beef, roast	5.20	22
corned, tinned	3.34	35
Chicken, white flesh, roast	1.60	31
red flesh, roast	2.70	24
Mutton, roast	5.10	24
Veal, roast	1.35	55
Bacon, raw	2.50	29
Pork chop, fried	1.40	47
Tongue, cooked	5.80	19
Rabbit, stewed	1.89	42

IODINE

Only a very minute amount of iodine is needed by human tissues, the daily requirement being given by Professor V. H. Mottram as 75 micrograms, which is 75 one-millionth part of a gram[2]. Iodine is, however, essential for the correct functioning of the thyroid gland. This gland controls the rate of metabolism and that of normal growth in children. Lack of iodine causes the thyroid gland to enlarge, a condition recongnizable as goitre. An enlargement of the gland happens during pregnancy and lactation, when additional iodine is needed, and food containing iodine should be especially included in the day's meals. Children need additional iodine during adolescence.

Drinking water should contain traces of iodine – except in those areas where the soil in iodine-free – as will milk taken from cows which feed on pasturage where the soil contains iodine. The richest sources are sea-foods – fish and the edible seaweeds. Where iodine occurs in the soil, the watercress and onions grown there will be the richest vegetable sources.

SODIUM AND CHLORIDE

Sodium and chlorine are recognizably taken as table salt and constitute that element in salted foods. This combination element – sodium chloride – is essential in the production of healthy gastric juice and a good digestion. Its function in the blood is to assist in carrying carbon dioxide to the lungs. Most people eat far more salt than they need, and since the body has difficulty in absorbing the coarse division of most salts taken with food, sodium chloride deficiency is not uncommon. Biochemic preparations of salt for the table are to be preferred to the use of a coarse table salt and molecular doses of *Nat-m.* can adjust an imbalance in the body tissues and fluids (See *Nat-m.,*).

Those who are engaged in heavy work which induces considerable sweating, who take strenuous exercise, or who live in hot climates, require a higher salt intake. If any of these conditions induces muscular cramps, it is a symptom that too much salt has been lost from the body and a saline drink is indicated.

It has been estimated that adults need 4 grams of salt daily and the average intake has been given as 15 grams; the body normally excretes excess salt in the urine and through the sweat.

POTASSIUM

Potassium has an affinity for the muscle cells and in the blood becomes a constituent of the red blood cells. It is not lost in sweat and is excreted only in the urine, approximately, three grams daily being lost this way. Most foods contain potassium, except tripe, tapioca, sago, fats and the processed starches – such as arrowroot, polished rice. These foods have little or no patassium content. Good sources of potassium in foods are given below:

	mg. per oz.[3]
Cod, steamed	102
Mutton chop, raw	100
Beefsteak, raw	95
Herring, raw	90
Milk	71
Eggs	39
Cheddar cheese	33
Cornflakes	32

SULPHUR

Human tissues need *sulphur*. The inorganic element is an essential factor in carrying oxygen more particularly to the skin. Sulphur occurs as a protein compound and eggs and fish are the best sources, vitamin B_1 and whole-grain proteins also contain this element.

MAGNESIUM

Magnesium is found in almost all foods. This mineral is a constituent of the bones and teeth, it nourishes all nerve tissue and in association with calcium and phosphorus it gives elasticity to muscle tissue. Magnesium promotes ease and relaxation of nervous tension and those who are troubled with symptoms of acidity may need remedial doses of this mineral.

MANGANESE

Manganese is related to the iron content in human tissues, and a dilution as a nutrient will increase the iron in the blood and tissues. Manganese is found in nuts, whole-grain cereals and teas.

TRACE ELEMENTS

Fluorine

So very minute an amount is required by the human body of *fluorine* that this becomes a "trace" element. It is essential in the composition of sound bones and teeth, and apparently the advisable intake is 0.3–0.5 parts of fluorine per million. This marginal figure should give good results only and produce excellent teeth. Larger amounts are likely to cause a mottling of the teeth and poisoning results – as is the case with "trace" elements – when this element occurs in excess.

Fluorine is a constituent of most drinking water, and the content is generally in strict control.

Copper

Copper is an essential "trace" element is human tissues, necessary for the formation of hemoglobin, and acting as a catalyst, that is, it produces a required chemical reaction without which the necessary process would not be activated. Its function in this connection is to keep up the number of red corpuscles in blood, preventing anemia.

Copper also assists iron in blood as a carrier of oxygen to the tissues. Many foods contain a trace of copper and the best sources are liver, nuts, peas, beans, beans, fruits and green vegetables.

Zinc

Zinc is found in most of the foods. It is an essential element of the body's production of insulin and is required for regulating sugar metabolism. It also assists blood in carrying carbon dioxide to the lungs for elimination.

WATER

Water is an essential nutritional factor. It is the major constituent of blood and digestive juices, and the food can only be absorbed in solution. The body eliminates aproximately 4½ pints each day, and this replacement is obtained in the proportions of about one-third from solid food, ½ pint from the assimilation of this food and the remainder – 2–3 pints of fluid is taken in the form of various drinks. In conditions of fever and diarrhoea, a higher intake of fluid is needed and natural water is the best choice to give. Those who take strenuous exercise or who live in hot climates will require a higher intake of fluid to compensate the increased loss from greater perspiration.

REFERENCES :

1.   0.09 oz. of iron, and 0.00009 oz. of iodine.
2.   *Food Sense,* edited by Professor V. H. Mottram.
3.   Figures given in *Manual of Nutrition,* published H.M.S.O.

CHAPTER 6

Vitamins in Food

VITAMINS are accessory food factors producing necessary chemical reactions in association with related elements. Thus, the presence of vitamin D in association with calcium and phosphorus is the essential factor in effecting the chemical reaction for calcium-phosphorus absorption in the human tissues. Similarly, vitamin B_{12}, having the trace element cobalt within itself, is vitally important in pernicious anemia. (Cobalt is frequently the vital link in the iron-cobalt-copper chain of elements required in blood making)

Vitamins are present in natural foods before they are purified for experimental purposes or for popular taste or have been subjected to second-rate cooking processes or – as is particularly the case with vitamin C – largely lost in the staling and bruising of the living plant.

When food is persistently taken which does not contain the full complement of these vitamins and the essential minerals, mild or serious conditions of deficiency soon become apparent and subnormal health and disease result. In these cases, eating those foods which contain a sufficient quantity of these necessary factors is of major assistance in restoring optimum health.

Each vitamin necessary for human nutrition has its own particular function, but some are in close relation to their nutritional processes. This is so of vitamins A, C and D, which are all associated with calcium and phosphorus intake in promoting growth of bone structure and the renewal processes in gastric juice, soft tissues and mucous membranes.

Where the community is reasonably well fed, any vitamin deficiency is most apparent in early spring after the lack of sunshine and young green vegetable produce sustained during the winter months. Most of the summer's vitamin D store within the tissues has been utilized unless it has been supplemented by especially chosen foods or vitamin capsules. Vitamin C is predominant in the sprouting points of green vegetables, for example, sprouting broccoli and in all young growing product. Some supplies of lettuce, cress and other salads are grown under glass, but the main crops come with spring. Garden and wayside herbs too, do not have their full content of vitamin C before they start into their spring growth. Part of the necessary vitamin C content in food can be obtained from fresh fruit and from summer supplies that have been suitably bottled for winter use.

Unhealthy conditions of the bowel, particularly diarrhoea, cause loss of vitamins and mineral nutrients. The use of medicinal paraffin, especially if taken soon after food, will carry through the bowel both its contents and the vitamins there which have not been given time for intestinal absorption, even supposing the natural secretions and micro-organisms of the colon are sufficiently active to promote this essential nutrition.

The important vitamins for human well-being are the fat-soluble A, D, E and K, and those which are water-soluble, the vitamin B complex and vitamins C and P.

VITAMIN A

In vitamin A we have essentially a protective factor, since where the intake of this vitamin is inadequate, human tissues easily take infectious diseases. This vitamin has a special relation with all the epithelial tissues, the lining cells which protect all organs and body tissues, and a deficiency of the vitamin results in poor stamina of these protective cells. This is seen in easy infection to cold, influenza, measles, bronchitis, gastric influenza, mumps, diseases in which the protective tissues of the skin, the eyes, the lungs, sinuses, the digestive organs and the glands are variously involved.

A serious deficiency of vitamin A results in deterioration and consequent ulceration of the membrane of the eyes, with blindness, if the condition is not corrected in time.

Exhaustive research work has established the amount of this vitamin needed daily by the various sections of the community. Adults and children in their "teens" require 5,000 International Units, but a youth of eighteen years or so will require 6,000 I. U. This figure has also been arrived at for the expectant mother, but during lactation her requirements are increased to 8,000 I. U. Young children of two years or more will need 2,000 I. U., but at five years they need more than 2,500 I. U. per day.

There are two forms of this vitamin in food. That which occurs in vegetable product is known as the vegetable vitamin A and from animal, fish or dairy products as the animal vitamin A. More of the intake of the vegetable vitamin A is used in the actual assimilation of this food factor, more from some vegetable sources than others, and it is generally estimated that only one-third of the intake from this source is available to the tissues. The recommendation is the proportion of one-third of the animal vitamin and two-thirds of the vegetable vitamin.

This vitamin is not destroyed by cooking or the process of canning.

The body does not use more vitamin A than it needs, but any additional intake is stored in the liver and then used later against a seasonal deficiency.

Vitamin A in Food

It is difficult to give exact figures of vitamin A content in various foods since appreciable variation is shown from the samples tested, and in the figures given by two such undoubted authorities as Professor V. H. Mottram in *Food Sense* and H. M. S. O. Publication, *Manual of Nutrition.* There is quite a wide seasonal variation, the vitamin content in milk and butter falling low during the English winter compared with the high vitamin content when animals are fed on a rich pasturage. Soil conditions and the amount of sunshine probably account for variations in the figures from the vegetable sources. The following figures appear to be valid:

Animal A	*I.U. per oz.*
Ox liver	4,255
New Zealand butter	1,140
English butter, summer	1,000
English butter, winter	255
Cheese, Cheddar	369
Eggs	280
Kidney	280
Condensed milk (whole milk)	105
Sardines	70
Herrings	42
Fresh milk, summer	195
Fresh milk, winter	8

Halibut liver oil	600,000
Cod liver oil	30,000
Vegetable A	
Parsley	3,690
Spinach	3,000
Turnip tops	2,130
Carrots	1,730–5,197
Kale	1,570
Dried apricots	1,420
Tomatoes	800
Dried prunes	600
Watercress	475–1,418
Cabbage	180

Small amounts of the vitamin are contained in fresh apricots, peaches, plums and greengages, and green peas. The dark green leaves of vegetables contain more of this vitamin, carotene, than the inner and paler leaves.

Vitamin A is synthetically added to margarine. The figures given by Professor Mottram are 450– 550 I.U. per oz. and in the H.M.S.O. publication, 850 I.U. per oz., which indicates a wide variation in the samples tested.

VITAMIN D

The function of vitamin D is so closely related to calcium and phosphorus metabolism that it has been dealt with discussing those elements. Foods which contain this vitamin again show a seasonal variation, and almost the only natural sources are:

	I. U. per oz.[1]
Halibut liver oil	5,400–114,000
Cod liver oil	5,670
Sardines	280
Herring	250
Tinned salmon	170
Eggs	17
Butter	3–28
Cheese	4–10
Milk	0.3
Margarine has the vitamin added synthetically	90

VITAMIN B COMPLEX

Vitamin B complex consists of food factors especially affecting the nervous system and the metabolism of carbohydrates. If the end-product of this metabolism, glucose, is not properly oxidized – through B_1 vitamin – these products circulate in blood and poison the nervous system. The amounts needed of this vitamin are in relation to the amount of carbohydrate eaten. Whole grain foods are good sources of the vitamin and more than balance their carbohydrate content. Meats contain this vitamin, and fruits and vegetables balance their carbohydrate contents. Yeast preparations and wheat germ foods are excellent sources of the vitamin.

Taking sulphonamide drugs renders this vitamin and the microbes which synthesize it in the body inactive.

Vitamin B_2 generally known as *Riboflavin*, is especially vital to the body's digestive processes. An insufficiency in the daily meals over a period of time causes nervous depression, easy infection to disease, skin becomes unhealthy and the vision suffers. Generous amounts of this vitamin bring robustness to children. It is a catalyst, a reactive agent in the assimilation of food products and increases growth in children.

Nicotinic acid is the third of these B vitamins; it is called *Niacin* in America. A slight deficiency of this vitamin is not at all uncommon. The symptoms include a red, sore tongue, with diarrhoea and abdominal pain, accompanied by lassitude and depression. Natural sources of this vitamin are yeast, whole-grain foods, meat and offal, mushrooms, peanuts, eggs, herrings, white fish and beer.

The other vitamins of this group are *Pyridoxine, Pantothenic acid, Biotin, Folic acid, Choline, Paramino-benzoic acid, Inositol* and *vitamin B_{12}.* With the exception of the Folic acid factor and vitamin B_{12} they are of secondary importance in general nutrition as they are usually found in flours which contain the germ and the husk, in natural unpolished rice, in milk, eggs and vegetables; a number of these foods are normally included in daily meals.

The Folic acid factor is vitally important in certain forms of anemia, and is found in the leaves of green vegetables and salads, in yeast, in liver and in kidney, and meals specially inclusive of these foods need to be given to sufferers with this disease.

Vitamin B_{12} is unusual as it contains the trace element, cobalt. Research on the nature of this vitamin continues. It is claimed that B_{12} restores the blood picture to normal in pernicious anemia and has a good effect on the accompanied disability of the nervous system. This is most probably effected by the presence of the trace element cobalt within the vitamin.

B_{12} is apparently the only vitamin in the B group which the body is able to store. The liver is able to do this since B_{12} is in combination with a protein and an enzyme. This compound prevents pernicious anemia.

All conditions of diarrhoea and taking purgatives interferes with the activity of the B group of vitamins; similarly, while sulphonamide drugs are being taken. Sunlight destroys the Riboflavin content in milk when it is left so exposed.

Only a little of the B_1 and Riboflavin vitamin are lost in dry cooking processes, but the alkalis in baking powder and raising agents destory some of the vitamin content while making cakes and scones. The B_1, Riboflavin and Nicotinic acid easily dissolve in cooking liquids, but if a small amount of this liquid is used to make soup or gravy enriched with these vitamins, the whole is then used at the meal.

Daily Requirements of Vitamin B

The daily requirements for this vitamin group by the various sections of the community are different for the seperate vitamins.

The intake for B_1 needed by sedentary workers is atleast 1.1 milligrams each day; an active adult needs atleast 1.5 milligrams; an expectant mother 1.8 milligrams; and a very active man and the nursing mother require atleast 2.0 milligrams daily. A child of 2 years needs 0.6 milligrams, at 5 years the requirement is 0.8 milligrams and at 14 years, 1.3 milligrams is needed; a youth of 18 who engages in strenuous sport will need atleast 1.8 milligrams.

The requirement for Riboflavin (vitamin B_2) is about half as much again as for vitamin B_1 for each of the various sections of the community. Some part of this is manufactured within the tissues of healthy subjects, but it is estimated that the daily requirement is from 1.6 to 2.6 milligrams according to age and occupation.

The requirement for Nicotinic acid is atleast 12–20 milligrams a day. It is advisable to increase this during pregnancy and lactation. The activity of microbes in the large intestine, both manufacture and destroy the vitamin. If much energy is expended and a larger amount of food consumed, a higher figure for intake is needed to provide the link in the metabolism of carbohydrates taken.

As will be seen from the table of natural sources, yeast and yeast products provide the highest content of these vitamins.

Natural sources of vitamin B_1.[2]

	mg. per oz.
Dried brewer's yeast	2.75
Bacon	0.17
Oatmeal	0.13
Green peas	0.12
Peanuts, roasted	0.07
Wholemeal bread (100% extraction)	0.07
Mutton	0.05
White bread	0.04
Potato	0.03
Beef	0.02
Cabbage	0.02
Milk	0.01

Natural sources of Riboflavin[2]

	mg. per oz.
Dried brewer's yeast	1.54
Liver	0.85
Cheese	0.14
Egg	0.11
Beef	0.07
Milk	0.04
Wholement bread (100% extraction)	0.03
Potato	0.02

Natural sources of Nicotinic Acid [2]

	mg. per oz.
Dried brewer's yeast	10.3
Liver, kidney	3.8
Beef	1.3
Bacon	1.1
Wholemeal bread (100% extraction)	1.2
Peanuts, roasted	0.6
Cod	0.6
Beer	0.4
Potato	0.3
White bread	0.3
Cabbage	0.1

VITAMIN C

This vitamin is also known as *Ascorbic acid*. Its presence in the body protects the tissues from scurvy. Symptoms of a slight deficiency in the intake of this vitamin occur frequently, for many people do not take sufficient foods which contain it. Symptoms of this deficiency are irritability, sore gums, tissues easily bruise, rheumatism-like pains in the joints, lack of stamina, slow or interrupted growth in children and lack of resistance to infection.

This vitamin is associated with vitamins A and D and the minerals calcium and phosphorus in the balance of metabolism in human tissues, promotion of good bone structure and healthy teeth. Vitamin C assists assimilation of carbohydrates and in the correct activity of heart and muscle tissue.

The presence of vitamin C promotes healing after surgical treatment, including the extraction of teeth. It is as well, a protective vitamin in neutalizing the poison from the tuberculosis germ. In addition, it assists the absorption of iron.

Research indicates that adults need atleast 20 milligrams of this vitamin daily; American standards aim at 75 milligrams daily. Sufferers of rheumatoid and those with any fever are likely to need 40 to 50 milligrams daily. Elderly people seldom have enough of this vitamin.

Health suffers from even temporary shortages of this vitamin. This is particularly likely to happen in late winter months and early spring before the young salads and sprouting vegetables are in good supply. There is a higher vitamin C content in the growing points of green vegetables, and in the young growing leaves of chives and dandelions than when mature; the skins of oranges, tomatoes and apples have a higher content of the vitamin – provided these fruits have been recently gathered – than the pulp. Loss of the vitamin occurs as the skin shrivels. The highest content of the vitamin is in growing stage just before coming to maturity or ripening. Stored foods gradually decrease in their vitamin content, whether these be green vegetables, roots or fruit.

Special Care Against Loss of Vitamin C

Vitamin C is the most susceptible of all the vitamins to loss. This occurs from the action of its own plant substances and shown in withering, fading, bruising. Loss also occurs in prolonged heating, as in baking, boiling, etc. The vitamin is easily soluble and there is considerable loss when vegetables are left steeped in cold water for more than a short period.

Loss of this vitamin occurs if it comes into contact with copper pans and if soda is added in cooking green vegetables. Exposure of vegetables to sunlight, once they have been cut and gathered, and keeping milk standing in sunlight, results in loss of the vitamin.

While preparing vegetables for a meal some cell damage is unavoidable. Bruising, cutting, peeling, grating, all cause cell damage. This releases a plant enzyme which, when in contact with oxygen destroys vitamin C. The lesser the cutting and the sharper the knife, the less will be the cell damage and vitamin loss. All vegetables should be used as soon as possible after the necessary cell damage has occurred, for if they are left standing, further loss of the vitamin continues through the enzyme action.

If vegetables are cooked in their skins, it saves vitamin loss. If the water in which green vegetable are to be cooked has reached boiling point, this temperature ensures that the enzyme itself is destroyed before it destroys the vitamin.

Less cooking time is required if vegetables are coarsely cut and if the roots are cut it large pieces, and by using the minimum water for the process, there is less continued cooking loss. In addition, the content of the minerals and the vitamin leached out into the cooking water will be contained and can be used as a vegetable broth and served as a small drink before the meal. This drink can be enriched with a yeast preparation.

Vitamin C Loss In Fruit

Fruit is protected by its skin and its own acids, and suffers much less loss of its vitamin C than vegetables, though bruising and damage should be avoided. Fruit should be kept cool to sustain its peak perfection just previous to being fully ripe. If fruit has to be cut for later use at table, a light sprinkling with lemon juice prevents further vitamin loss and deterioration.

There is little loss of vitamin C in cooking the fruit and if a little water is added, the cooking juice is also consumed. The addition of bicarbonate of soda to fruit for any purpose destroys its vitamin C.

Sources of Vitamin C in Foods	milligrams per oz. of the raw food[3]
Blackcurrants	57.0
Oranges	16.0
Strawberries	16.0
Grapefruit	14.0
Lemon	12.0
Melon	8.5
Raspberries	9.0
Loganberries	9.0
Pineapple	5.7

Cherries, grapes, pears and plums	1.0
Peppers	35.0
Chives	33.0
Brussels sprouts	28.0
Cauliflower	20.0
Cabbage	20.0
Sprouting broccoli	18.5 and higher
Watercress	17.0
Kohlrabi	14.0
Swedes, turnips	7.0
Tomatoes	7.0
Lettuce	4.0
Spring onions and French beans	3.0
Celery	1.0

VITAMIN P

This vitamin is found in close association with vitamin C and has been called vitamin P because it gives permeability to the fine blood vessels. Where there is a lack of this vitamin, the blood seeps through the walls of these small vessels and shows in the surrounding tissues as if these had been bruised.

Many vitamin C foods also contain this vitamin like, black-currants, tomatoes, summer cabbage and lettuce, and rosehip syrup; other fruits which have little or no vitamin C have a good content of vitamin P – apples, plums and cherries. A good variety of these foods should provide adequate supplies of both these vitamins.

No figure for the daily requirement of vitamin P for human beings has yet been fixed.

VITAMIN E

The human requirement for vitamin E is not yet known and research in connection with this vitamin continues. It is thought that it has some influence on cholesterol metabolism and possibly an anti-thrombotic effect.

This vitamin appears to be closely associated with the reproductive system and has been found useful with other measures in preventing habitual abortion, during menopause, to prolong maturity and avoid ageing of the tissues.

Good natural sources of the vitamin are wheat germ, lettuce, egg-yolk, milk.

VITAMIN K

Vitamin K is essential to enable the blood to clot and is an anti-hemorrhagic vitamin. The vitamin is found in green vegetables and in green peas. If the meals contain sufficient supplies of vitamins A and C, this vitamin should automatically be included. There is another substance normally manufactured in the large intestine having this same K activity, called K_2 and if for some reason vitamin K should be absent *temporarily* from the food intake, the body should have this second protective factor within its tissues.

Taking medicinal paraffin or other similar laxatives is likely to impede the manufacture of K_2 within the body.

REFERENCES :

1. Both Professor Mottram's figures and the H.M.S.O. *Manual of Nutrition* have been consulted.
2. These figures are given in H.M.S.O. *Manual of Nutrition*.
3. This analysis given in *Food Sense,* edited by Professor V. H. Mottram.

CHAPTER 7

Therapeutic Section

Note: *Certain diseases are notifiable to the authorities as constituting a source of infection or danger to life. Biochemic treatment can be followed in all conditions of pain and disease at the discretion of the individual concerned, but the laws of each country in these matters must, of course, be complied with.*

INDEX OF TREATMENTS

APPENDICITIS

Give *Ferr-p.* and *Kali-m.* alternately, in half-hourly doses in 6X or 3-200X potency, with four doses of *Mag-p.* in 3X or 3-200X potency, during the first day of illness. Give also two doses of *Silicea*[1] in 3-200X potency, during the day. Apply hot fomentation, using four doses of *Ferr-p.* in a small solution.

During subsequent days of illness, give *Ferr-p.*, and *Kali-m.* in 12X potency or 3-200X potency in two hourly doses and repeat the two doses (morning and afternoon) of *Silicea* in 3-200X potency.

Continue the hot fomentations if they are needed.

No food must be given. Give only tepid water to sip. The bowels can be cleansed with an enema using a pint of warm water, provided this can be taken comfortably by the sufferer.

If a putrefactive bowel appears to be the cause of appendicitis or is a contributing factor, *Kali-p.* must also be given, at hourly intervals in 12X or 3-200X potency.

If *peritonitis* is threatened, having a tympanitic abdomen (drum-like), give half-hourly doses of *Kali-s.* in 12X or 3-200X potency, in addition to the doses of *Ferr-p.* and *Kali-m.* as detailed for appendicitis. However, give *Kali-p.* instead of *Ferr-p.* if fever persists.

ARTHRITIS AND RHEUMATISM

Arthritis having some degree of deformity – use *Silicea* and *Calc-f.* in 30X potency or 3-200X and take one dose of each, morning and evening.

The "crippled" tissues are able to absorb the high potency of these tissue salts and the fibre cells regain some elasticity and strength. In some cases, full regeneration is possible, but this depends on several factors, such as age and weight and if the tissues involved have been subjected to continued use and strain.

Where this disease has been present for some years and these remedies need to be used for some time, it is advisable to omit the doses entirely, say, on Sundays and on Wednesdays.

In chronic and long standing conditions of this disease, compound prescriptions incorporating essential trace elements as synergists may be needed.

The daily meals need to be well balanced and little salt should be taken as this is likely to upset the valuable sodium potassium balance in the tissues. (See also Appendix for comments and menus under Rheumatism and Arthritis.)

RHEUMATISM

Inflammatory Conditions

With soreness or pain in the muscles or within a joint, generally with swelling and stiffness. The pain is worse on movement of the muscle or joint, and the longer the movement is continued the worse the pain becomes.

Use *Ferr-p.* and *Kali-m.* in alternation in 12X potency or 3-200X; if the condition is acute, take five doses of each salt during the day and as the condition improves take the doses less frequently.

Oxygen-deficient Rheumatism with Weakness

Joints feel weak, standing is disliked; the pain is worse when warm in bed or in warm rooms and in the evenings; pains move around and are in muscles and joints. (Some irregular function of the glands is usually present and foods containing iodine are needed. See chapter on iodine.)

Use *Kali-s.*, use also *Mag-p.* in alternation if the sufferer is a highly-strong person, usually tensed up or if the pains are usually worse on the right side of the body. Use 12X potency or 3–200X, morning and evening, of one or both remedies and more often if the condition seems specially acute.

Toxic and "Acid" Rheumatism

Brings pain on movement, but the condition is easier with continued movement. The pain and difficulty in movement is usually worse in the early part of the day, or after a period of rest.

Use *Nat-p.* and *Kali-p.* in alternation, both in 12X potency or 3-200X, three times a day between meals.

Nat-p. is the tissue remedy to emulsify the degenerated lactic acid in the tissues causing the pain and *Kali-p.* is the remedy for the secondary toxic conditions present in this type of rheumatism.

This condition is usually worse in damp weather or if living in damp conditions, when a dose of *Nat-s.* in the same potency should be taken in addition each day this is relevant.

Systematic and Chronic Rheumatism

Take one dose of *Silicea* daily, in 12X or 3-200X potency.

In damp weather also take one dose of *Nat-s.* in 12X or 3-200X potency.

If the condition becomes acute with heat and swelling in any part of the body, see *Inflammatory rheumatism;* See also comments and dosage for *Toxic* and *Oxygen-deficient rheumatism.*

Refer also to comments on food and the daily menus.

See Appendix for details of relative trace elements; How to understand Rheumatism and Arthritis; Three Food Dangers; Foods and Menus for use in Rheumatism and Arthritis.

BLOOD DISORDERS

Abscess, Boils

Give *Ferr-p*. and *Kali-m*. alternately, both in 6X or 3-200X potency and at hourly intervals.

Give also *Silicea* in 12X or 3-200X potency, three doses a day.

When the abscess or boil discharge and continue so without healing, change the remedies to *Calc-s*. and *Nat-s*. alternately, both at two-hourly intervals, using 12X or 3-200X potency.

If, however, the discharge becomes putrid and foul-smelling, give frequent doses of *Kali-p*. in 3X or 3-200X potency.

Additional rest may be needed and food which contains plenty of fresh fruit and vegetables with sufficient assimilable iron and vitamins B and C. (See chapters on these foods)

Hot fomentations should be applied. Bathe the external parts with a solution of the remedies, using fresh lint at each application. To make this solution, use 3 doses of the remedy, internally in half a cupful of hot water. The solution and the fomentation should be hot but reasonably comfortable for the patient.

Carbuncles

Use the same treatment as for abscess and boils. In addition, take two doses daily of *Calc-f.* in 12X or 3-200X potency.

Gangrene

If a condition becomes gangrenous or if there is a fear that this may be so, give *Kali-p.* in any potency available, preferably 12X or 3-200X, at frequent intervals. Give also *Kali-s.*, *Silicea* and *Ferr-p.* in the same potency, in half-hourly doses.

BRONCHITIS

Acute Condition with Fever

Use *Ferr-p.* 6X or 3-200X, a dose every half-hour until the temperature has returned to normal.

All cases of bronchitis are likely to benefit from *Ferr-p.* since it carries oxygen to the lung tissues and assists in expelling morbid materials; except in the case of fever, as above, take a dose of *Ferr-p.* twice a day in 12X or 3-200X potency.

Chronic Conditions

With a dry, painful cough, use *Nat-m.* $12X^2$ or 3-200X, three times a day and *Ferr-p* as above, twice daily.

With loose, frothy phlegm, use *Nat-m.* $12X^2$ or 3-200X, three times a day and *Ferr-p.* as above twice daily.

With thick and white or grey phlegm, use *Kali-m.* 12X or 3-200X, three times a day and *Ferr-p.* as above, twice daily.

Chronic bronchitis of some years standing may need a prescription of *Kali-m.* or *Kali-s.* to be supported with trace elements, to assist the debility of the weakened tissues.

All sufferers with bronchitis need to check if they are having sufficient vitamin A in their daily food.

Suitable massages can be of great benefit in chronic bronchitis. It increases the patient's strength and general nutrition, and exercises should be given, according to the age and strength of the sufferer, for improving the circulation and general mobility of the thorax. This treatment is to assist expectoration and respiration and act as a tonic to the lung tissues. The breathing exercises must especially help expiration.

Abdominal massage should usually be included, unless there are contraindications, and it is often of much benefit.

CATARRHS

Nose and Throat

Acute Catarrh

With thick, white phlegm or these nasal exudations, use *Kali-m.* 3X or 3-200X, every hour till relieved.

Acute and Heavy Catarrh

With thick, yellow mucus, sometimes accompanied by picking of nose, give *Nat-p.* 6X or 3-200X, two or three doses at hourly intervals.

Chronic Catarrh

Slight and watery, take *Nat-m.* and *Calc-p.* alternately, each twice a day, in 12X or 3-200X potency.

If discharge is creamy-yellow, take *Nat-p.* 12X or 3-200X, twice a day before meals.

If the discharge is offensive, take *Kali-p.* and *Silicea* alternately, 12X or 3–200X, each twice a day, between meals.

If mucus is greenish, use *Nat-s.* 6X or 3-200X, at hourly intervals until it has altered – requiring another tissue remedy– or cleared.

Itching or dryness of the edges or the tip of the nose, indicates a need for *Silicea*. Use 12X or 3-200X, twice a day. If the nose is icy cold at its extremity, take *Calc-p.* 12X or 3-200X, twice a day.

Catarrh of the Vagina

See Leucorrhea.

CHILLS AND COLD

If chilled, with shivering and cannot get warm, take *Ferr-p.* 3X or 3-200X; a dose every 15 minutes. And if possible, go to bed wrapped in a blanket, with a hot water bottle.

Many chills are satisfactorily thrown off by taking a few doses of *Ferr-p.* only, but to be efficacious, this remedy should be taken promptly.

At the first sign of having a cold – the throat is sore – take *Ferr-p.* 3X or 3-200X, frequently.

For a feverish cold, with a high temperature, take *Ferr-p.* 3X or 3-200X, approximately every half-hour while awake. A sleeper with high temperature should not be wakened, but given the remedy on coming naturally out of sleep.

While the temperature is above normal, nothing should be eaten, a little cold water to drink or fresh orange juice.

A blanket bath is advised. The patient, otherwise naked, is wrapped loosely in a blanket, a sponge or face flannel is immersed in cold/cool water and wrung almost dry. Within cover of the blanket ligthly and quickly wipe the whole body with this flannel

–first one side of the body, then the other, using a rolling action and adjusting the blanket. Then wrap closely with the blanket and cover well with the usual eiderdown and blankets. The patient may be expected to perspire freely and sleep. After several hours the patient will wake, feeling much better, and the temperature will be lower. It is not likely the temperature will go up and down, it will steadily come down.

When the temperature has returned to normal, 98.4° or 99.0° at the very most, freshly made weak tea can be given if desired. On returning to a normal temperature, and some patients go subnormal, a little bread and butter or toast should be given, preferably using brown bread to help the bowel action and provide the needed vitamin B. A few hours later, check for a steady temperature at normal and then light meals using dairy produce, fruit and vegetables can be resumed.

Watery Stage of Colds, etc.

For watery running of nose or eyes or other part of the body, take *Nat-m.* 3X or 3-200X, hourly with *Ferr-p.* every two hours in the same potency.

Mucus Conditions

Where there is a clear, jelly-like mucus or greyish-white phlegm or a nasal exudation of similar description, take *Kali-m.* 6X or 200X, three doses daily.

If the mucus or phlegm is thick and white or rather yellow, take *Kali-s.* 12X or 3-200X, three times a day.

If the mucus is hard and knotty, take *Silicea* 12X or 3-200X, three times a day.

For dryness at the back of the nose, take *Nat-m.* 3X or 3-200X, hourly.

For the sensation of stuffiness or of being "stuffed up" , take *Kali-m.* 12X or 3-200X, hourly.

If a *hacking cough* has developed, take *Kali-m.* 12X or 3-200X, four or five doses a day.

If the presence of phlegm causes *coughing,* but nothing is expelled, take *Silicea* 12X or 3-200X, three or four times a day.

If spasms of *tickling cough* develop, take *Mag-p.* and *Silicea* alternately, in 6X or 3-200X, during such spasms.

In all cases, frequently *breathe out deeply.*

CONSTIPATION

If the anus is dry and retentive, and all efforts at stool come to nothing, use *Nat-p.* at half-hourly intervals until the condition is easier and a bowel motion results; 6X or 3-200X potency.

If the bowel motion is difficult and dry, take *Nat-m.* for several days, a dose at bedtime and again in the morning, in the 6X or 3-200X potency.

If the bowel motion produces hard knotty stools, take *Nat-s.* for several days, at bedtime and early in the morning in 6X or 3-200X potency.

If there is no motion and the tongue is yellow, take *Kali-s.* for several days, at bedtime and early in the morning in 6X or 3-200X potency.

If the stools recede and there is difficulty in expelling them, take *Calc-f.* and *Silicea*, a dose of each at bedtime and again early in the morning, 6X or 3-200X potency.

If there is no bowel action and the tongue is white, take *Kali-m.* for several days, a dose at bedtime and again in the morning, in 6X or 3-200X potency.

If there is no desire to attend stool, take a dose each of *Kali-p.* and *Calc-f.* at bedtime and again in the morning for several days, in 12X or 3-200X potency.

If there seems to be inflammation or heat, or pain in the bowel, take *Ferr-p.* every half-hour in 6X or 3-200X potency, until the condition is relieved.

It is necessary to fix a time to attend stool as this assists in re-establishing satisfactory habits. Individuals vary in their needs as to whether this should be once, twice or thrice daily.

In all cases of difficult bowel action, it is advisable to see that the meals contain enough vitamins, calcium and assimilable iron.

It is *highly important for good health* that the bowels show a healthy activity.

If the tissue remedies are taken as indicated for the various conditions of this trouble, natural and healthy motions should result within a short space of time. If the diet is deficient in its essential factors, referred to above, this should ofcourse be adjusted at the same time. In some cases sufficient exercise may not be taken. In these circumstances, a daily walk or some indoor exercises and abdominal breathing should be undertaken.

Purgatives and laxatives containing medicinal paraffin oil are detrimental to the bowel and should not be used. Such measures interfere with intestinal absorption of vitamins and essential food products, and weaken all natural bowel activities.

DEAFNESS

If this is accompanied by inflammation, giving heat and pain or internal swelling localized close to the ear, give *Ferr-p.* alternated with *Kali-m.* in 12X or 3-200X potency, in hourly doses of each, and then less frequently as the acute condition improves.

If the deafness is primarily due to a nervous cause, use *Kali-p.* and *Mag-p.* alternately in 12X or 3-200X potency, each every two hours *Mag-p.* is better taken in hot water.

If the deafness is worse in the evening, with noise in the head, accompanied by a slimy tongue and possibly yellowish exudation, give *Kali-s.* in 12X or 3-200X potency, evening doses at two hourly intervals.

If there is hard matter in the ear, which causes deafness, use *Calc-f.* and *Silicea* alternately, in 3X or 6X or 3-200X potency, doses every 15 minutes. If this does not clear the condition within an hour or so, professional advice is needed.

For general chronic deafness, the chief remedies are *Kali-m., Kali-p.* and *Silicea*, used alternately, in 12X or 3-200X potency or 30X potency, if the patient is elderly, two doses a day of each. Sufficient vitamins A and C need to be given in the daily meals.

Deafness is sometimes occasioned by bone changes, when skilled professional advice may be of assistance.

DIARRHOEA

If the diarrhoea is of greenish stools, take *Nat-s.* hourly, in 6X or 3-200X potency.

If the diarrhoea is of stools containing blood and slime, take *Kali-m.* hourly, in 6X or 3-200X potency.

If the diarrhoea is slimy, yellow, take *Kali-s.* hourly, in 6X or 3-200X potency.

If the diarrhoea is because of a chill, use *Ferr-p.* depending on this condition as to the dosage being taken (probably half-hourly), 3X or 6X or 3-200X potency.

If the diarrhoea is fetid smelling, take *Kali-p*. 12X or 3-200X, three times a day.

If the diarrhoea contains frothy water and is slimy, use *Nat-m*, 6X or 3-200X, hourly.

If the diarrhoea smells sour, is brown, liquid and watery, use *Nat-p*. hourly, in 6X or 3-200X potency.

If the diarrhoea shows undigested food, use *Ferr-p*. hourly, in 12X or 3-200X potency.

FEMININE DISORDERS

Dysmenorrhea (Painful Menstruation)

Use *Mag-p*. and *Calc-f*. alternately, both in 6X or 3-200X potency, take hourly doses, with additional doses of *Mag-p*. in hot water for spasms of pain or for convulsive pain.

If the menstrual blood is dark and clotted, use *Kali-m*. instead of *Calc-f*. in the same potency and frequency.

If the discharge during the latter part of the period becomes yellowish-brown, use *Kali-s*. in 12X or 3-200X potency, three doses during the second half of each day.

For subjects who are soon nervously depleted, take three doses of *Kali-p*. each day towards the latter part of the period, and in 12X or 3-200X potency.

Menorrhagia (Heavy Menstrual Flow)

Use *Ferr-p., Calc-p*. and *Kali-s*. alternately, take three doses of each daily, in 6X or 3-200X potency.

May be accompanied by inability to relax or by a deficiency of *Calc-f*. in the glands, and the tissue remedies will quickly put this right. *Menorrhagia* indicates a mineral deficiency in the daily meals, notably of calcium and iron.

In both conditions where constipation is a factor, this of course needs attention.

If these measures have not established a normal and reasonably comfortable condition, it is advisable to seek skilled advice.

Leucorrhea (the "Whites")

If the discharge is transparent and rather gelatinous, use *Calc-p.* in 6X or 3-200X potency, and take three doses a day; if the discharge is white, take *Kali-m.* in the same potency, three times a day; if it is yellow is color and stales to brown, take *Kali-s.* in the same potency; if it is a golden, creamy yellow take *Nat-p*; but if the discharge is watery, take *Nat-m*. In all cases, the same potency and frequency of doses can be adhered to.

The condition is usually one of debility, sometimes of a catarrhal nature, and plenty of fresh air, some exercise and sensible meals which include plenty of fresh vegetables, salads and fruit are needed.

Menopause

If menopause brings digestive disturbance or feeling of heaviness or sluggishness, take *Nat-p.* and *Kali-s.* one dose of each in the morning and evening on alternate days in the week; and more frequently if symptoms of an acid or irritating discharge is causing inconvenience or distress.

If flushings and hot waves occur, take *Ferr-p.* every ten minutes while these continue. A dose of *Kali-p.* is also advised.

If nervously inclined, take a dose of *Kali-p.* each day until this condition has improved.

A potency of 6X or 3-200X is suitable in all these remedies of the above conditions.

If there is be occasional periods of menorrhagia, use the remedies as given for this condition.

Plenty of fresh air, a daily walk, good breathing exercises, light food which contains an adequate intake of assimilable iron and vitamins, and freedom from anxiety, are measures which should ensure a natural, easy development from one period to life of the next.

FEVERS

High Fevers

Symptoms of fever with high temperature – use *Ferr-p.* every fifteen minutes until the temperature gradually drops, lessening the frequency of the dose to hourly and two hourly intervals. A 6X potency will ordinarily be used, but if the condition gives 102° or more (except in a child), a 30X potency will be needed. Children easily run a high temperature and 6X potency in their case should be correct.

If *Ferr-p.* does not suffice to bring the temperature down gradually, and particularly if the sufferer has a highly nervous temperament, give *Kali-p.* in 3X potency. As soon as there is an improvement, alternate *Ferr-p* with *Kali-p.*

(If 3-200X potency is being used, one potency is given of both the remedies in all circumstances.)

If, subsequently, the fever is under control but the temperature rises in the evening to any degree, then give *Kali-s.* 6X or 3-200X, in two doses of two hourly intervals.

A gentle but quick sponge-over with a flannel or sponge squeezed out of cold/tepid water while the sufferer is between blankets assists the control of the temperature and gives a relief to the patient. Wrap the blanket around the patient afterwards and cover suitably.

If the bowel is *temporarily* inactive in feverish chills, after about thirty six hours *Nat-m.* should be given. (See treatment for Constipation)

Low Fevers

With symptoms of severe chilling, cannot get warm, subnormal temperature, nausea or vertigo, intermittent and bilious fever, chilling with vomiting or diarrhoea, influenza with gripe.

Give *Nat-s.* and *Kali-p.* in 3X or 3-200X potency, both in half-hourly doses until the temperature is normal, the sickness, vertigo and gripe have lessened; if the temperature then runs high, give *Ferr-p.* in 6X or 3-200X potency.

When the acute stage has passed, give these three remedies, preferably in 6X or 12X or 3-200X potency, each three times a day.

Specific Fevers

Brain Fever

With delirium, use *Ferr-p.* and *Kali-p.* alternately, a dose of each remedy at approximately half-hourly intervals, in 12X or 3-200X potency, and *Nat-m.* in the same potency, every two hours.

Chickenpox (Infectious)

Give *Ferr-p., Kali-m.* and *Nat-m.* in alternate doses throughout the illness, in 6X or 3-200X potency, unless very severe give a dose of each remedy every two hours for the first two days, and then three times a day.

Diphtheria

Characterized by grave throat symptoms and the formation of patches of congestion on mucous surfaces, highly infectious. For the slight fever, the stiffness of the neck and the swelling of the glands at the jaw angle, give *Ferr-p., Kali-m.* and *Nat-p.* alternaterly, each remedy every two hours, in 12X or 3-200X potency. In addition, use all three remedies as a compound gargle, several times daily.

If there is exhaustion, give *Kali-p.* in 3X or 6X or 3-200X potency, in half hourly doses until there is an improvement.

If the patches of congestion on the throat spread, forming a membrane down the larynx causing difficulty in breathing, give *Kali-m.* alternately with *Calc-p.* in 12X, 30X or 3-200X potency, every half-hour.

If watery diarrhoea or vomit is present during the illness, give *Nat-m.* in 12X or 3-200X potency, hourly until the condition has improved.

Similarly, if greenish, watery diarrhoea or vomit is present give *Nat-s.* in same potency and frequency until this condition has improved.

A cautious and protracted convalescence is necessary. Any constipation will need attention.

Glandular Fever (Infectious)

Sudden stiffness of the neck, inability or difficulty in swallowing and fever. After three days, the cervical glands become enlarged and tender; debility and constipation. (See treatment for constipation.) The glands do not suppurate; convalescence is often slow.

For the fever give *Ferr-p.* in 6X or 3-200X potency, probably every hour, unless the fever becomes sharp and runs high, when more frequent doses will control it; give less frequent doses as soon as the fever is down to 100° or 101°. A soon as the glands become swollen, give *Kali-m.* in 6X or 3–200X potency, every two hours.

The bowels should be kept active and the patient should rest in bed. A light, nourishing diet is suitable as soon as the temperature has become normal. When the swelling of the glands has subsided, change from *Kali-m.* and give *Calc-p.* and *Ferr-p.* alternately, in 12X or 3-200X potency, three doses of each daily, to assist convalescence.

Hay Fever, Sinusitis

Acute

Use *Ferr-p.* and *Nat-m.* alternately in 3X or 3-200X potency, half hourly until relieved.

Chronic

Use *Nat-m.*, *Silicea*, *Kali-p.* each two-hourly in alternation, from two days, and then twice daily in 12X or 3-200X potency.

In severe cases, a compound prescription which has included trace elements has proved effective.

Skilled manipulative treatment is generally of considerable benefit, particularly if given with these remedies.

Influenza

For the *"ache"*, where there is an aching all over, take *Nat-s.* 3X or 3-200X every half-hour. This should break up the aching.

If chilled, use also *Ferr-p.* alternately, 3X or 3-200X.

Fever

If the temperature rises, leave *Nat-s* and take only *Ferr-P.* 3X or 3-200X every half hour. If possible, go to bed, wrap in a blanket, and have the treatment as for a feverish chill with a blanket bath.

Nothing to eat until the temperature has dropped to normal; drink cold water or fresh orange juice.

This is the normal and safe way to get well quickly.

If there is much wateriness from the nose, eyes, etc., use *Nat-m.* 3X or 3-200X, every two or three hours.

Use *Kali-m.* and *Kali-s.* alternately for the convalescent aches, tiredness and drained feelings; 12X or 3-200X, each twice a day, and a dose of *Kali-p.* 12X at bedtime.

Gastric Conditions

If at the commencement of the illness, gastric symptoms are predominant, take *Nat-s.* and *Nat-p,* alternately, 3X or 3-200X, each every half-hour, and less frequently as the condition improves.

If gastric symptoms (pain, nausea) continue in some degree throughout the illness, take one dose each of *Nat-s.* and *Nat-p.* at night and in the morning, using 12X or 3-200X potency.

Measles (Infectious)

Symptoms include sudden, running discharge from the nose and eyes; rash on the fourth day on forehead and face, with increased fever for about a week.

Give *Ferr-p., Kali-m.* and *Kali-s.* Use *Ferr-p.* while there is fever, and also if the temperature rises again when the rash appears. (With these remedies this will most probably be slight.) Use 6X or 3-200X potency as in high fever.

If wateriness of the nose and eyes is present, give *Nat-m.* at two-hourly intervals, and the same potency.

If the cough or catarrh develops, use *Kali-m.* and do so after the rash has appeared and developed; give three or four doses a day in 6X or 3-200X potency.

When all signs of fever have subsided and the rash has faded, give *Kali-s.* to clear the subsequent skin condition, in the same potency, three times a day. *Ferr-p.* should not be needed now.

If at any time during the illness catarrhal diarrhea is present with green offensive stools, give two or three doses of *Nat-s.* in 6X or 3-200X potency, at two hourly intervals.

If constipation is present, see treatment under this heading.

Mumps

(Infectious before the glands are affected and for two to three weeks after.) Symptoms include pain under one ear with stiffness or soreness of neck and jaw, with fever, usually 101°–103° or more; swelling of the parotid gland, which is tender and elastic to pressure; mastication and swallowing are very painful, foul breath, furred tongue. Both sides of the neck may be involved and the swelling form a collar or first one side is affected and then the other. As soon as the swelling subsides there is rapid improvement; the glands rarely suppurate.

The bowels should be kept active from the beginning of the illness. (See treatment for Constipation). An antiseptic mouthwash is helpful and hot fomentation should be applied to the swellings. Male patients need to be kept in bed for about ten days, against the possible risk of orchitis.

Between the fomentations, a light scarf should be worn to keep the effected parts warm. (Do not give hot fomentations while the fever is running.)

Give *Ferr-p.* for the fever in 6X or 3-200X potency, every half-hour while this is acute and then less frequently as soon as it is under control. As soon as the swelling appears, give *Kali-m.* 6X or 3-200X, four doses daily, alternately with *Nat-m.* in the same potency, until all pain, stiffness and swelling have gone, and the tongue is normal

If the fever is very high, a blanket bath should prove a relief to the sufferer. (See treatment of High Fever)

Rheumatic Fever

Symptoms include moderately high temperature with general soreness and stiffness, and rheumatic pain in one of the larger joints. The affected joint is red, hot, swollen, with much pain later the redness subsides and the joint becomes dead white in appearance. There is marked sweating with sour odour, the tongue is large, flat and thickly furred. The urine is scanty and high colored.

Give *Ferr-p.* and *Nat-p.* alternately, in 6X or 3-200X potency, both remedies at half-hourly intervals and less frequently as the fever subsides and the condition improves.

For the sharp, shooting pains use *Mag-p.* in that same potency and in hot water, also half-hourly until these have subsided. If there is local swelling around joints, use *Kali-m.* and *Nat-p.* alternately, in 12X or 3-200X potency, and at two hourly intervals. If, however, there are watery symptoms, use *Nat-m.* and *Nat-p.* instead in 12X or 3-200X potency and at two hourly intervals. If the pains move about from one place to another, use *Kali-s.* in the 12X or 3-200X potency, at two hourly intervals.

Scarlet Fever (Infectious)

The symptoms are vomiting, pains in the back and limbs, sore throat, high fever and headache, rapid pulse; the glands at the jaw angle swell; a rash on the chest which spreads over the face and body.

If the temperature is high, give *Ferr-p.* in 12X or 3-200X potency, half-hourly, also give *Kali-m.* in 12X or 3-200X potency at two hourly intervals, with *Kali-s.* in the same potency in the evening at two hourly intervals.

Kali-s. promotes the needed development of the rash and the subsequent peeling of the skin; it is given to cure any dropsy that may be present.

If there is stupor or extreme exhaustion during the illness, give *Kali-p.* in 12X or 3-200X potency; also if the throat becomes *sore and putrid.* In these circumstances the doses can be inserted inside the lower lip; repeat half hourly until the condition has improved.

While the temperature is high, no food should be given, only cold water or juice from a squeezed orange should be given to drink.

Throughout this illness only *protein* food should be given in minimum quantities to relieve the strain on the kidneys.

Give a daily toilet with tepid sponging and if the bowels are inactive, give the indicated remedies. (See treatment for Constipation)

If the illness is slight or aborted, the symptoms will be slight and may escape notice except for later skin eruptions or some nephritis.

Tonsillitis

For the hot, dry throat and high temperature, give *Ferr-p.* internally and as a gargle. Use 6X potency or 3-200X, and give a dose every half-hour and then hourly as soon as there is an improvement. For the gargle, dissolve three or four doses in half a cup of warm water. Give a cold compress to the frontal headache.

See that the bowels are acting freely and keep them so during the illness. (See treatment for consipation).

As the illness develops, for the enlarged glands and swollen tissues, give *Kali-m.* and *Nat-p.* alternately, in 12X or 3-200X potency, three or four doses of each a day, and now only one or two doses a day of the *Ferr-p.* If there is difficulty, now, in using a gargle, the throat can be sprayed with *Kali-m.* made up as a gargle, which is excellent for this purpose.

If *quinsy* develop, give *Silicea* in 12X or 3-200X potency, three doses a day.

During convalescence, the meals should contain foods rich in calcium, iron and vitamins.

There may be difficulty in diagnosis in distinguishing between acute tonsillitis and diphtheria. In tonsillitis, the fever is generally high, with the throat also hot and the headache is severe; in diphtheria, the fever symptoms are generally slight.

Typhoid or Typhus (Infections)

Intense headache, nausea, temperature rapidly runs up, vomiting, rigors and pains all over the body, pupils are contracted, tongue thickly furred, constipation, exhaustion, noisy delirium, eyes and face suffused; rash on the fifth day beginning on the abdomen, the upper part of the chest, hands and wrists, and later the rest of the body.

For continous high fever *Kali-p.* in a high potency, 12X or 30X or 3-200X, every hour, or every two hours if the sufferer is elderly, give also *Calc-p.* in the same potency twice a day.

If fluid is present in the tissues give *Nat-m.* in 12X or 3-200X potency, two of three doses a day.

If a rash has developed, give *Kali-s.* in 12X potency or 3–200X, three doses a day.

Throughout the illness an evening dose of *Kali-s.* is advised in 12X or 3-200X potency.

If constipation is present, for treatment, see under Constipation.

FIBROSITIS

(Treat as for chronic rheumatism). Take one dose of *Silicea* daily, 12X or 3-200X.

Use *Ferr-p.* 6X or 3-200, for any acute inflammatory condition – heat, swelling and pain in any part of the body – at hourly intervals until the condition is better.

In damp weather, one dose of *Nat-s.* is also of benefit; 6X or 3-200X.

Skilled manipulative treatment is of great benefit, also, if this is available.

If an inflammatory condition persists, as it sometimes happens in the trapezius or the intercostals, use *Kali-p.* rather than *Ferr-p.* to deal with the toxic condition which has localized and is causing the inflammation. Breathing-*out* exercises are advised to assist in clearing some probable congestion of the liver and to improve the digestion by the elimination of used carbonic acid gas from the tissues.

INJURIES

Immediate Injuries

To mitigate shock and bleeding, give at once *Kali-p.* and *Ferr-p.* together, in a little water or dissolved in one's own saliva; introduce the solution or thin paste inside the lower lip on the tongue of the injured person. Frequent doses at ten minute intervals, and then less frequently as needed, using any potency rather than none, but preferably 3X or 6X or 3-200X.

Neglected Injuries

If festering, use *Silicea* 6X or 3-200X, but if continuing sanious use *Calc-s.* instead in the same potency, using the remedies, three times a day until easier.

Bites and Stings

Take internally *Nat-m.* 3X or 6X or 3-200X, also *Silicea* and *Kali-p.,* if severe, in the same potency. Doses every ten minutes. For subsequent swelling use *Kali-m.* instead of *Nat-m.* in 12X or 3-200X potency, if available, three or four doses a day. *Also,* use these remedies as a lotion in paste form, with the saliva. *Kali-p.* has an antiseptic quality. Renew the lotion as it dries off.

Bleeding and Cuts

Take *Ferr-p.* internally at ten minute intervals, until bleeding subsides. If parts swell, then use *Kali-m,* three or four doses a day, lessening doses as the condition improves. If parts are torn or lacerated, use *Kali-p.* also.

The dressing should be soaked also in a solution of *Ferr-p.* together with *Kali-p.* if it is being used. Bandage well over this dressing. The solution can be renewed through the dressing without removing this.

Nose-bleed

Use *Ferr-p.* and *Kali-p.* taken internally at ten minute intervals until bleeding stops, in 3X, 6X or 3-200X potency. If, however, the bleeding is black and clotted, use *Kali-m.* instead at similar intervals and in the same potency.

Blood Poisoning

Use *Nat-m.* and *Kali-p.* internally, 12X or 3-200X, probably four times a day, as needed; use these remedies also as a solution on dressing where applicable.

Bruises (Flesh)

Use *Ferr-p.* for the inflammation and *Kali-m.* for any swelling, in potency of 3X, 6X or 3-200X, taken internally at ten minute intervals until better, and subsequently two or three times a day if still necessary.

Use the same remedies as a cool lotion with a lint dressing under a bandage.

Bruises of the Shin, Ribs, etc. (Bones)

Use a lotion of *Calc-f.* on lint under a bandage or suitable dressing.

Burns and Scalds

Use *Ferr-p.* and *Kali-m.* internally, at ten minute intervals, 3X or 3-200X. A solution of *Kali-m.* on lint can be given to prevent blistering. For this purpose do not remove the lint dressing, but add the lotion to the lint and cover with another piece of lint. It is now recognised, however, that these injuries are generally better kept as dry as possible.

Kali-p. should also be given for shock, internally, 3X or 3-200X, at suitable intervals for an acute condition.

Head Injuries –Falls, Blows, Concussion

Use *Ferr-p.* and *Nat-s.* internally, inserted as a thin wet paste with the saliva into the mouth or inside the lower lip, using 3X or 3-200X. Repeat at fifteen minute intervals until the condition has improved, if the concussion is serious and gives little response give the doses three or four times over twenty four hours and use a higher potency.

Treat any external bruises or cuts with the indicated remedies under these categories.

Hernia and Rupture

Take *Calc-f.* and *Silicea* alternately, in 6X or 3-200X potency. Apply a cold compress over the swelling and preferably soaked first in a solution of *Calc-f.* Keep the knees raised.

Patella (Knee-cap) – Injured by Falling

Use *Calc-f.* in 6X or 3-200X potency, internally and as a lotion on lint; dose and apply every thiry minutes until the conditon is better, and then two or three times a day, preferably in a higher potency. Rest the leg with a cushion under the knee to keep it slightly flexed.

In case of fracture, it will need to be set.

Sprains with Inflammation

Use *Ferr-p.* internally and as a lotion, in 6X or 3-200X potency, internally every ten minutes to commence with and then hourly, renew the lotion as it dries off.

For the swelling, change from *Ferr-p.* to *Kali-m.* in the same potency, both internally and as a lotion, at hourly intervals.

Rest the injured part.

Strain

Take *Kali-m.* and *Calc-f.* alternately, in 6X or 3-200X potency, at hourly and then two hourly intervals.

Rest the injured part.

Sunstroke

Give *Nat-m.* dissolved as a paste with the saliva placed on tongue or inside lower lip, with a cold water compress against the *top* of the head and across the forehead.

INSOMNIA

If the sleeplessness is *occasional* or *intermittent* and if from working late in the evening, from worry or excitement (nervous causes), take *Kali-p.* 30X or 3-200X, about an hour before retiring, on getting into bed and should this be necessary, another dose one hour later if still awake.

If from a feeling of pressure of blood to the head (congestive) take *Ferr-p.* in 30X or 3-200X potency, and at intervals as given above.

If with stomach discomfort or with symptoms of acidity (digestive), heartburn, creamy tongue, creamy exudation at the corners of the eyes, take *Nat-p.* 6X or 3-200X, at intervals as given above.

If the sleeplessness is *persistent* and the above remedies do not suffice, a trace element is probably needed in the prescription. There may also be over-fatigue and a need for more exercise and fresh air than is being obtained, particularly towards the end of the day. The meals should contain sufficient vitamin and mineral intake. Skilled manipulation of the neck and head tissues is of value in relieving congestion and improving the circulation to the brain.

If the sleeplessness is caused by weakness of the heart muscle and indicated by hearing the heart beat when lying on the left side, take *Calc-f., Kali-p.* and *Nat-m.* in 12X or 3-200X potency, one dose of each remedy at bedtime and again in the morning until the condition has improved.

LUMBAGO
From Chill

Take *Ferr-p.* in 6X or 3-200X potency, frequently, with alternate doses of *Kali-m.* in 3X or 3-200X potency and *Nat-p.* in 6X or 3-200X potency, each remedy will need to be taken hourly. A hot-water bottle against the affected part gives comfort.

Suddenly, from Strain with much Pain and Binding of Muscles

Take *Calc-f., Mag-p.* and *Calc-p.* in 6X or 3-200X potency, every twenty minutes for the first two hours, and then a dose of each remedy once every two hours. *Mag-p.* is best taken in hot water and if 3-200X potency is used, take three times the ordinary dose each time.

Skilled manipulative treatment, if available, usually puts the matter right very quickly.

NASAL CONDITIONS

Itching or dryness of the edges or the tip of the nose indicates a need for *Silicea*. Use 12X or 3-200X, twice a day.

If the nose is icy cold at its extremity, take *Calc-p*. 12X or 3-200X, twice a day.

Offensive Discharge

Give *Kali-p*. 3X or 3-200X, hourly. (In nervous subjects nose-bleed may also occur or frequent sneezing)

Persistent Sneezing (with Chill)

Use *Ferr-p*. and *Nat-m*. alternately, 3X or 3-200X, every half hour until better.

Polypus

Take *Calc-p*. 3X or 3-200X, three doses a day. See also that the daily vitamin D intake is adequate; a vitamin supplement may be necessary. Every opportunity should be taken for sensible exposure to the sun's rays.

Sense of Smell

If lost, try *Mag-p*. 12X or 3-200X. If diminished, use *Kali-s*., *Silicea* and *Mag-p*. alternately, each three times a day in 3X or 3-200X potency.

Sense of Stuffiness

Use *Kali-m*. 3X or 3-200X, four times during the day or night.

Ulcerations

Inside the nose, surface ulceration, in children, give *Calc-p.* 3X, three doses a day.

Deep ulceration, in adults, discharge corrodes, give *Silicea* 12X or 3-200X, three times a day; syringe or bathe with a solution of same in warm water.

NERVOUS DISORDERS

Nervous Depression

Take *Kali-p.* in 3X or 3-200X potency, at hourly intervals.

Hysteria

Give *Kali-p.* in 3X or 3-200X potency, every ten minutes.

Nervous Exhaustion with Irritability

Take *Kali-p.* and *Nat-p.* in 3X or 3-200X potency, every ten minutes.

Obsessions, Neurosis, Mania

Give *Kali-p., Mag-p.* and *Nat-p.* three doses of each daily, in 12X or 3-200X potency and one dose of *Silicea* daily in 12X or 3-200X potency.

Nervous

Give *Kali-p.* and *Mag-p.* in 6X or 3-200X potency, frequently for immediate treatment; three times a day in 12X or 3-200X potency for prolonged conditions and for delayed nervous shock, with a dose of *Silicea* once a day in the same potency.

If the condition is accompanied by constipation, try giving *Nat-m.* twice a day in the same potency and increase the intake of vitamin B foods in the meals.

Nervous Vertigo

Take *Kali-p.* in 3X or 3-200X potency, but if with biliousness; take *Nat-s.* instead in the same potency; frequent doses until normal.

Sea and Travel Sickness

Take *Nat-p.* and *Kali-p.* in 12X or 3-200X potency, two doses before starting and during the travel; at half-hourly intervals if the condition becomes acute; but at two hourly intervals as a preventive.

This procedure has been found excellent.

Trembling, Shaking or Giddiness From Inside

Take *Kali-p., Ferr-p.* and *Mag-p.* in 3X or 3-200X potency, two doses of each within a few minutes of each; continue. further doses if necessary.

Where There is Hesitancy and Shrinking from Work from Nervous Debility or from Nervous Shock

Take *Kali-p.* once a day, and *Ferr-p.* and *Silicea* three times a day, in 12X or 3-200X potency. See that the meals contain sufficient mineral and vitamin content.

NEURITIS

Take *Ferr-p.* and *Kali-p.* alternately. If the condition has come on suddenly and is acute, 3X or 3-200X potency should be used every fifteen minutes, then half-hourly, and each remedy every two hours as soon as the pain has lessened.

If there are pressure points on the nerve from rheumatism in a neighbouring joint (usually the shoulder) or the humerous is out of alignment with pressure on the nerve and limitation of movement of the arm, these are indications that skilled manipulation and suitable massage is required.

The addition of *Nat-p.* in 12X or 3-200X potency, several doses daily, will assist in clearing any rheumatic congestion present.

PILES (OR HEMORRHOIDS)

With low back pains, constipation and itching, take *Calc-f.* in 12X or 3-200X potency; use also as a lotion.

If bleeding with bright blood, use *Ferr-p.* in 12X or 3-200X potency; use also as a lotion.

If bleeding with dark clotted blood, use *Kali-m.* in 6X or 3-200X potency, and as a lotion.

If there are sharp darting pains, use *Mag-p.* in 6X or 3-200X potency.

If piles are accompanied by a feeling of heat in the descending colon or rectum, take *Nat-s.* in 12X or 3-200X potency.

If the condition is acute, take half-hourly and hourly doses; if chronic, three and four doses a day are advised.

If the condition is general, see that the meals contain sufficient calcium and iron. And if constipation is a feature or the daily movements need assistance, see the section on Constipation.

SCIATICA

An excruciating pain along the course of the sciatic nerve running from under the buttocks to the knee. Take *Kali-p.* 3X or 3-200X, every fifteen minutes, half-hourly and hourly as the condition improves. If the pain is shooting, with spasms, take also *Mag-p.* in the same potency, preferably in hot water.

If there is some contraction of the muscles of the affected leg, take also *Nat-m.* in the same potency.

If accompanied by rheumatism, take several doses of *Nat-p.* in 3X potency if this is acute and in a higher potency or 3-200X if this is a constitutional tendency.

If the sciatica proves obstinate, take *Silicea*, *Ferr-p.* and *Calc-p.* alternately, three times a day, each in 12X or 3-200X potency.

(*Note:* The bowels should be active and in obstinate conditions there may be pelvic congestion which needs specific attention)

SKIN DISORDERS
Acne and Pimples

With inflammation of the skin, take *Ferr-p.* and *Nat-p.* 3X or 3-200X potency; if with hard matter, take *Calc-p.* and *Silicea* in 3X or 3-200X potency.

If the acne is slow to heal, remaining moist and yellow, take *Nat-s.* in 3X or the 3-200X potency.

If young people, also give *Calc-p.* in 3X or 6X or 3-200X potency.

In each case, three doses a day.

(*Note:* See that the meals contain a good content of calcium, assimilable iron and vitamin C)

Alopecia

The chief remedy is *Kali-p.* in 12X or 3-200X potency, three doses a day, with rest from nervous worry.

Other remedies may be needed constitutionally, in support – *Nat-m.* or *Kali-s.* in 12X or 3-200X potency, one or two doses a day.

Corns

Take *Kali-m.* and *Silicea* both remedies in 3-200X potency, three times a day.

If these are present on the feet, bathe the feet daily, change the hosiery frequently and have well-fitting shoes, exercise for the feet, a few minutes twice or thrice a day without shoes on are in any case helpful for improving the circulation and the condition of feet.

Chaps and Cracks of the Skin

Nat-m. and *Calc-f.* should be taken in 12X or 3-200X potency, three doses of each every day for a short period.

Dandruff and Dryness

Take *Kali-s.* and *Nat-m.* in 12X or 3-200X potency, two doses of each every day for a period of two to three weeks.

Eczema

After vaccinations– take *Kali-m.*; if eruptions are watery, use *Nat-m.*, but if these have yellow, watery secretions use *Nat-p.* and *Nat-s.* alternately.

If the eruption brings irritation, take *Kali-p.* and *Nat-p.* but if there is redness with burning pain take *Ferr-p.* and *Nat-p.*

In all these conditions a 12X or 3-200X potency is advised, three doses a day.

Inflammation (and Redness)

The first remedy for any inflammation of the skin is *Kali-m.* Take frequent doses of the 6X or 3-200X potency.

Ringworm on Body or Scalp

Give *Kali-m.*, *Kali-s.*, *Nat-p.* and *Silicea* in 6X or 3-200X potency, three doses of each every day.

Shingles of Herpes

Take *Kali-p.* and *Nat-m.* alternately, each three times a day in 6X or 3-200X potency. If the temperature usually registers as subnormal, add a dose each day of *Nat-s.*, preferably in 12X or 3-200X potency.

Two doses each day of *Calc-p.* and of *Ferr-p.* should be taken also as a tonic in 3-200X potency.

(*Note:* The meals should be rich in calcium and assimilable iron foods, and in vitamins B and C; refer to these sections)

Warts

Take *Kali-m.* and *Silicea* alternately, in 3-200X potency, three times a day; add *Nat-s.* in this potency, twice a day if the constitution is bilious.

STOMACH DISORDERS

Acidity

Take *Nat-p.* in 3X or 3-200X potency, frequently and a daily dose of *Ferr-p.* in 12X or 3-200X potency.

(See that the meals contain sufficient assimilable iron in the foods chosen)

Biliousness

Rest from food. Take *Nat-s.* in 3X potency frequently; twenty four hours later fresh weak tea and dry biscuits (Vita-wheat, digestive, or home-made) are usually suitable; and *Kali-m.* in 6X or 3-200X potency, three doses a day, with *Nat-s.* in the 12X or 3-200X potency, one dose a day.

Gastritis

Rest from food. Take *Ferr-p.* and *Kali-m.* alternately, in 6X or 3-200X potency, both remedies hourly; and for the nervous exhaustion take *Kali-p.* in the same potency, at two hourly intervals.

Heartburn

Usually needs *Ferr-p.* and *Nat-p.* alternately, in 6X or 3-200X potency, frequent doses.

Bilious conditions, however, will probably need alternate doses of *Nat-m., Nat-s.* and *Silicea*, frequent doses in the same potency.

Rest from all food for a short period until the condition is cured.

Ulceration of Stomach

Take *Kali-p.* and *Nat-p.* in 3X or 3-200X potency, at half-hourly intervals and within five minutes of the first remedy for acute conditions. Take two hourly doses for chronic conditions.

It is usually advisable to feed those with this condition with milk, and fruits and vegetables, until the condition has healed.

Worry and anxiety need to be resolved to obtain the best and lasting results.

(A fasting regime is likely to produce anxiety and is not considered suitable for this condition)

Indigestion (Dyspepsia, Gastric Disorder)

Stomach tender, red tongue, vomit shows undigested food; take *Ferr-p.* in 6X or 3-200X potency, half-hourly and rest from all food; drink cold water in sips.

If there is flatulence, with sharp spasms or cramps in the stomach, take *Mag-p.* in hot water, 3X, or three doses at once of 3-200X; repeat at frequent intervals while the condition lasts.

If there is excessive flatulence with heart discomfort and pain, take *Calc-f.* and *Kali-p.* alternately, in 3X or 3-200X potency, at frequent intervals while the condition lasts.

If the tongue is greyish-white, sometimes with pain under the right shoulder, take *Kali-m.* in 6X or 3-200X potency, at hourly intervals; if this does not shortly improve the condition, take also *Calc-s.* in the same potency, five minutes after the dose of *Kali-m.*

If the indigestion comes from a sense of fullness, usually worse in the evening, take a doses of *Kali-s.* in the early afternoon and early evening, in 12X or 3-200X potency.

If there is discomfort after eating fat or starch, take *Kali-m.* in 6X or 3-200X potency, three doses at hourly intervals and reduce the intake of these foods.

If there is a bitter taste after taking food, rest from eating and take several doses of *Nat-s.* in 3X or 3-200X potency, at hourly intervals.

URINATION

Retention

Take *Mag-p.* in hot water, in 3X or 3-200X potency, frequently until the condition is normal. This is generally from nervous causes or direct suppression.

In children it is probably from chill and *Ferr-p.* should be given in 3X or 3-200X potency, frequently until normal.

Frequent or Copious

The *Nat-m.* and *Nat-p.* alternately in 12X or 3-200X potency, twice a day.

Scalding

Take *Ferr-p.* and *Kali-p.* alternately, in 6X or 3-200X potency, three doses a day.

Burning

Take *Ferr-p.* and *Nat-m.* alternately, in 6X or 3-200X potency, three doses a day.

Interrupted, with Inflammation

Take *Ferr-p.*, *Kali-m.*, *Nat-s.*, three doses of each daily, in 12X or 3-200X potency.

Very painful, accompanied by the passing of mucus, pus, blood – take *Kali-p.*, *Silicea* and seek specialized advice. These remedies will probably be needed in 12X potency, three times a day.

Incontinence

From weakness of muscles – take *Ferr-p.* in 12X or 3-200X potency, three times a day.

From weakness of nerve – take *Kali-p.* in 12X or 3-200X potency, three times a day.

In children – give *Nat-p.* and *Kali-p.*, a dose of each in 3X or 3-200X potency, three times a day, until the condition is normal.

WORMS

If this condition is suspected, use *Nat-m.* and *Nat-p.* in alternation, in 3-200X potency, four doses of each daily.

Thread-worms

Use *Nat-p.* 3X and give an anal injection of four doses of *Nat-m.* 3X, dissolved in a small teacupful of warm water.

Others

Use *Nat-m.* in 12X or 3-200X potency, four doses a day, and *Nat-p.* and *Silicea.* in 12X or 3-200X potency, twice a day.

PAIN

It is often of composite character. Treat first its major factor, i.e. soreness or shooting pain or dull ache, etc. The following guide gives the relative Tissue Salts for reducing painful conditions. (Dosage: Half-hourly for acute conditions and then less often.)

Pain allied to swellings:	*use Kali-m.*
because of strains, hernias:	*Ferr-p.* & *Calc-f.*
colic and / or flatulence:	*Mag-p.*
cramp:	*Calc-p.* & *Mag-p.*
gastric pain and gripe:	*Nat-p., Mag-p.* & *Nat-s.*
headaches:	
cervical, back of head:	*Kali-s., Kali-m.* & *Ferr-p.*
frontal:	*Kali-p.* & *Mag-p.*
neck, shoulders, stiff or sting:	*see* fibrositis.
indigestion:	*Nat-p.* & *Mag-p.*
irritation of and under skin:	*see* skin disorders–shingles.
menstrual or muscle pains–dull aching:	*Kali-m.*
"pain and needles", numbness, with heaviness, stiffness:	*Kali-p.*
soreness, throbbing:	*Ferr-p.*
under shoulder blades or at points of shoulders:	*Kali-m.*

(When in pain, it is generally advisable to feed lightly to assist clearance of the liver)

REFERENCES :

1. The use of *Silicea* needs experience in this condition and may even be contraindicated.

2. Young sufferers can use 6X potency, four times a day. *All* elderly patients should also take a dose of *Silicea* each day, in 12X or 3-200X potency to strengthen the bronchial walls.

Appendix

TRACE ELEMENTS

Some sufferers with rheumatic and arthritic conditions need compound prescriptions of biochemic nutrients which incorporate certain trace elements. These trace elements have a special relation to the main constituents of the prescription and function as catalysts and synergists in achieving the required chemical processes of regeneration.

Advanced conditions are likely to need these compound prescriptions.[1]

HOW TO UNDERSTAND RHEUMATISM AND ARTHRITIS

Rheumatism and arthritis are classed as diseases of metabolism as distinct from virus infections.

The pains of rheumatism are felt in muscle tissues, in tendons and in inflammatory conditions of the joints; arthritis is an allied disease of the joints and bones.

The cells and intercellular fluids of the body depend upon the integrity of blood for nourishment, forming their individual patterns of composition and renewal. Too few minerals in food, insufficient vitamins, the wrong type of food and faulty assimilation, impoverish the blood and subsequently the fibres of muscles, membranes of bones and the articulations of joints. The electromagnetic quality inherent in body tissues attracts those forms of nourishment necessary for its health, generally by means of blood and lymph.

As well, the pattern-forms of all tissue are responsive to nervous and emotional stimuli, both from within the body and outside it. The stimulus of anxiety causes tense muscles, which if continuous prevents the full nourishment of these tissues and in turn the adequate dispersal of the waste products through the somewhat restricted circulation. If persistent, the result is either an inflammatory or a toxic condition; this may take the form of rheumatism.

Qualities such as confidence and contentment bring relaxation of mind and muscular tissues.

The use of the body beyond fatigue point brings undue wear and tear on those joints and tissues taking the stress of weight or friction, resulting first in inflammation, followed by degeneration of the articulations within the joint, which is a secondary process.

Nutritional deficiency is considered as a contributing cause in some rheumatic and arthritic conditions. The deficiency suggested is one of keeping the body's calcium organized, its proper laying down in the tissues and being in solution in the blood and digestive juices. And for the promotion of a correct calcium balance, sufficient intake of vitamin D is the main nutritional key. (See also calcium-phosphorus absorption)

Apparently calcium can be organized all through life, and this point should be of interest to many sufferers where calcium is out of balance.

Foods which are rich in potassium and sodium should also be included daily in the diet of those with rheumatism or arthritis, since these salts promote the correct fluidity of the cells and intercellular spaces of body tissues. A minute amount of iodine is another essential requirement, particularly where there is some disturbance in glandular function, which is often present in the oxygen-deficient type of rheumatism.

THREE FOOD DANGERS

There are three diet factors which need watching. The first is salt, the second is sugar and the third, the condition of the bowel.

The crude salt generally used in cooking, preserving and on the table is often taken in excess, and has been considered responsible by authoritative opinion for upsetting the body's sodium-potassium balance. Potassium acts as a *stabilizer* of the minerals and trace elements contained in healthy blood and tissues. Potassium is an inorganic chemical element of a compound nature and it is believed that crude salt displaces the values of its particles in relation to cell tissue, and is probably responsible for a number of serious diseases.

Little sugar is advisable for rheumatic sufferers, particularly those of the oxygen-deficient type. Sugar robs the body of its oxygen which it requires for its combustion in the tissues. Teas and coffee might well be taken without sugar, while honey and the dried fruits are advocated as better forms of sweetening where these can be used.

A healthy bowel promotes adequate vitamin and mineral absorption by the tissues. Where the natural secretions of the bowel and its own peristaltic action is insufficient to effect natural evacuations without additional stimulus, it is probable that the diet being followed is incorrect. The suggested menus should be tried for quite a period in an effort to establish a healthy condition.

FOOD AND MENUS FOR USE IN RHEUMATISM AND ARTHRITIS

Therefore, the meals of those who suffer with rheumatism or arthritis especially need to include foods which provide sufficient calcium and assimilable iron, and are a good source of iodine, potassium, sodium, vitamin D and its associated vitamins A and C, together with the intake needed of vitamin B.

Ofcourse, all these constituents will not necessarily be found in one or two foods, but a good variety of the right foods should provide these nutritional essentials.

Suggested menus for a week follow, which are designed to provide these factors, suitably mixed and attractive to personal needs. These meals will be found suitable for lacto-vegetarians, and those who eat fleshy foods.

A higher intake of dairy foods is generally advised and a correspondingly low one of fleshy food.

These menus cover general needs. They will not necessarily suit everyone and may have to be adapted to suit individual requirements. Quantities are not given, leaving freedom in this matter; but the general scheme should be followed reasonably closely.

MENUS FOR A WEEK

Breakfast

Dandelion Coffee[2] or Orange Juice or Tea, of approximately only three minute's standing. Darjeeling Orange Pekoe (a large-leaf, hill-grown tea) or Kenum China Tea or Matte Tea is suggested.

Four Days a Week

Orange jelly, using the juice of oranges, and made with carragheen[2] or agar-agar[2], served with one tablespoonful of a wheat-germ food[2]

or

Milk jelly, made and served as above

or

Jellied blackcurrants when in season, made and served as above.

Three Days a Week

Apple muesli with sliced raw, ripe apple, oats and a few blanched almonds, Barbados sugar, juice of half a fresh lemon and top of the milk.

or

Toast and butter if desired, using, preferably, 85 percent extraction flour.

The jelly and the muesli breakfast dishes can be served alternatively during the days of the week and so avoid mere repetition of the dish as a sweet course for later in the day unless personal choice dictates. The constituents of a dish may be similar (giving needed mineral or vitamin factors) but its treatment in preparation always gives some variety.

MID-DAY MEAL

A Salad Lunch with Cheese

Choose a comparatively lightly salted variety of cheese–

English Cheddar, Wensleydale, Caerphilly. If light protein cheese is needed, Cottage cheese or St. Ivel are recommended. Cream cheeses are rich in fat and light in protein, and these can be included for variety, with suitable adjustments to the rest of the meal.

The salad should contain as often as the season permits – dandelion leaves, cucumber (diced and to include the skin), chives, watercress, tomatoes, celery, beetroot, lettuce, parsley.

Watercress and the young dandelion leaves torn from the mid-rib should be used almost daily and obtained fresh that day. The other items can be used for variety during the week and include as an addition peas, turnips, spring onions, capers, nasturtiums, garlic.

A particularly good mixture, worth recommending for flavor, consists of watercress, dandelion leaves, parsley, chives and Caerphilly cheese.

The dry flavor of Wensleydale cheese blends well with a salad of celery, tomatoes or beetroot or cucumber, and watercress. Dress the salad if desired with olive oil and lemon juice.

Include boiled jacket potatoes at this meal

or

Bread and butter, using as near as possible an 85 percent extraction flour

The salad lunch can at all times be interchanged with the evening meal. In cold weather, salad meals should begin with celery, tomato or watercress soup or a hot drink made with a vitamin B extract, such as Yeastrel or Marmite.

MID-MORNING AND MID-AFTERNOON DRINKS

Dandelion coffee, made half milk, *or* a vitamin B drink *or* Tea of the varieties used for breakfast.

(No afternoon tea meal should be taken, nor cake or biscuits; the drink only)

THE EVENING OR COOKED MEAL

MONDAY

Cauliflower, cheese, carrots, peas, apple crumble.

TUESDAY

Grilled or baked fish – herring or white fish, with tomatoes and watercress and choice of vegetables

or

Sprouts and carrots with a nut dish

or

Spring greens, peas, and *Oeufs à la Normandie.*

(In this dish the eggs are poached and served with a little cream or cream cheese, which preferably should be added to the eggs during the last minute of cooking.)

Sweet of apple and orange salad with cream.

WEDNESDAY

Macedoine of carrots, celery, peas, turnips, potato and grated cheese, *or* egg and mushroom pie.

Sweet of wheat germ preparation and raisins, with cream or the top of the milk.

THURSDAY

Souffle, with kale, *or* cabbage, *or* young greens, and boiled or roast potatoes.

Sweet of rose apple tart.

FRIDAY

Omelette, *or* baked or grilled white fish, *or* tinned salmon.

French or runner beans, *or* green peas, potatoes.

Sweet of apple and sultana salad and cream *or* fresh fruits.

SATURDAY

Baked egg, onion and cheese dish with potatoes and watercress.

Sweet of orange jelly.

SUNDAY

Chicken *or* bucked egg[3] *or* roast lamb. Sprouts *or* sprouting broccoli *or* garden peas, and roast or boiled jacket potatoes.

Sweet of fruit salad.

In many cases the sunday cooked meal will be taken midday, and a late tea meal will follow in the early evening. Here bread and butter should be served with a green salad of dandelion leaves, celery, watercress, cress, chives, according to season, *or* sandwiches of the same, or of watercress and honey. Good home-made cakes, without sugar icing can also be served.

How to Make Watercress Soup

Details were published in *The Listener*, several years ago. Boil a pound of potatoes in just enough water to cover them, and add half-way through a bunch of well-washed watercress. When the potatoes are done, rub all through a sieve and season very lightly. It can be enriched just before serving with a little cream or top of the milk, but part of its attraction is its simplicity of flavor.

EVENING DRINKS

China tea, *or* dandelion coffee, *or* a vitamin B drink with milk, *or* a herb tea with honey, *or* Russian tea with lemon.

WINES

Sherry is considered unsuitable. It is a "plastered" wine, which means that at one stage of its production Calcium Sulphate is sprinkled on the grapes. This procedure has great antiquity. Its chemical effect is to produce an insoluble calcium in the wine which later "falls out", clarifying the wine but taking the phosphates with it, and increasing the free acidity of wine.

The free acidity and lack of phosphates may prove unkind to rheumatic sufferers.

A Marsala is suggested instead, or one of the liqueurs which includes herbs and fruits in its mixture, or a good home-made wine, such as dandelion or elderberry.

REFERENCES :

1. As far as is known to me, the British Biochemic Association are the only laboratories in this country who prepare specific compound prescriptions of these nutrients for the various conditions of these diseases.
2. These items are all easily purchasable from good grocers and health stores; they are attractive to the palate when correctly prepared.
3. In this dish a poached egg has the addition of a strip of plain cheese laid across the yolk and sprinkling of dried or fresh herbs.